Agriculture and Korean Economic History

Seong Ho Jun

Agriculture and Korean Economic History

Concise Farming Talk (Nongsa chiksŏl)

Seong Ho Jun
The Academy of Korean Studies
Seoul, Korea (Republic of)

ISBN 978-981-32-9318-2   ISBN 978-981-32-9319-9 (eBook)
https://doi.org/10.1007/978-981-32-9319-9

© The Editor(s) (if applicable) and The Author(s), under exclusive license to Springer Nature Singapore Pte Ltd. 2019
This work is subject to copyright. All rights are solely and exclusively licensed by the Publisher, whether the whole or part of the material is concerned, specifically the rights of translation, reprinting, reuse of illustrations, recitation, broadcasting, reproduction on microfilms or in any other physical way, and transmission or information storage and retrieval, electronic adaptation, computer software, or by similar or dissimilar methodology now known or hereafter developed.
The use of general descriptive names, registered names, trademarks, service marks, etc. in this publication does not imply, even in the absence of a specific statement, that such names are exempt from the relevant protective laws and regulations and therefore free for general use.
The publisher, the authors and the editors are safe to assume that the advice and information in this book are believed to be true and accurate at the date of publication. Neither the publisher nor the authors or the editors give a warranty, expressed or implied, with respect to the material contained herein or for any errors or omissions that may have been made. The publisher remains neutral with regard to jurisdictional claims in published maps and institutional affiliations.

This Palgrave Macmillan imprint is published by the registered company Springer Nature Singapore Pte Ltd.
The registered company address is: 152 Beach Road, #21-01/04 Gateway East, Singapore 189721, Singapore

To MyeongHee, PhillGoo and MinGoo

Preface

The historical context of the Miracle on the Han River refers to the transformation from one of the world's poorest countries to the global powerhouse following the Korean War (1950–1953), can be found in the fifteenth century transformed from a mediaeval commercial society to an early modern agricultural society. The resultant transformation had been attributed to the intensive work of the small peasants with enlightened Kings. The reign of King Sejong (r. 1418–1450) was a time period within world history with unprecedented advances in multiple areas. The technical publications compiled during his reign are also inextricably linked with the invention of the Korean alphabet as a national language system. In particular, Nongsa chiksŏl (農事直說) which can be translated into Concise Farming Talk (CFT) (also known as Straight Talk on Farming) can be regarded as the exemplar of reports on the new technological development industries led by the state.

After Korean War, the world order has changed an era of governance where the sovereignty over others has been weakened by emerging the sovereignty with others. In recent years, most of the countries have sought to enhance their traditional use of the sovereignty over others and have paid more and more attention to sovereignty with others. People open mind when eating food to get along with people, to talk with food and to get to know them better. Culinomics, which is an essential ingredient of human being, has always played an important role in power with others. Habitually, the sovereignty flies in the face of the paradox that Laos, Vietnam, and Korea are small and weak, but their Culinomics are excellent, but while the superpower, the USA and Russia, is viewed negatively in many countries of the world. This book wants to talk about what is "power with others"? How can "power with others" win "power over others"? This book raise King Sejong's sovereignty in the fifteenth century, his power always is with his people.

The Korean peninsula is mountainous and stretches mainly between 50 degrees and 30 degrees latitude, in a northeast-southwest orientation. The north of Korea is dominated by mountains, Paektu Mountain, also known as Changbai Mountain; Koreans call Hinmŏlli (hangŭl 힌머리) which means white-head like the Himalayan mountain. The name Himalayas is derived from Hindi term Himā-laya (हिमालय, Hangŭl 힌머리), and the definition of Himalayas in Oxford Dictionaries is "Abode of Snow," but the meaning is related to hangŭl 힌머리, which is the highest white-head mountain in Korea.

The mountainous area of northeast Asia and well-watered hilly places were the cradle of Korean civilization. The main story of this book starts with "Snow (The Hindi हिम, Hangŭl 힌눈)." Snow is very important icon for seasoned farmer's preparation of crop seed in Korea. The first chapter of CFT, "Preparing crops seed," states the well-being of the seed depended primarily upon an adequate snowfall during the winter.

The Altaic language family derives its name from the Altai Mountain region. The family of languages based on the mountain are originated from the Caspian Sea and Ural Mountains in the west to the Pacific Ocean in the east. The field of linguistic terminology changes from day to day, and new terms are continually being coined; for example, "Charming" in English etymologically means sense of "pleasing quality, irresistible power to please and attract" from Latin carmen related to religious formula.

There is a charming rice variety from Himalayas Central Indo-China, Laos, and Vietnam which is a relatively drought-resistant rice known as Champa rice also grown in Laos, Thailand, Cambodia, Vietnam, Malaysia, Indonesia, Myanmar, Nepal, Bangladesh, Northeast India, China, Japan, Korea, Taiwan, and the Philippines. An estimated 85% of Lao rice production is of this type. The rice has been recorded in the Korean Classics for at least 1,300 years. Sesame and buckwheat, which are also drought-resistant crops, are popular and essential ingredients in many Korean cuisines. In Korea, glutinous rice is called chapssal (Hangŭl: 찹쌀), and its characteristic stickiness is called chalgi (Hangul: 찰기).

Sesame oil called Charmchilŭm (Hangŭl: 참기름), Cooked rice made of glutinous rice is called chalbap (Hangul: 찰밥) and Champa rice cakes are called chalddeok or chapssalddeok (Hangul: 찰떡, 찹쌀떡). The meaning of "Charm" in Korean is "Truth" or "Real thing."

Jared Diamond (1997) hypothesized that if environment is important in limiting the spread of cultures, cultural units would also tend to extend more broadly along lines of latitude than along lines of longitude. However, the spread of CFT's crops tests Jared Diamond's hypothesis by comparing the range shapes. Champa rice in the mountainous area does not support his hypothesis: There is no significant tendency to expand more east–west than north–south.

This book can be taken as evidence that the fifteenth century was a historical paragon that heralded the path to the period of creativity aspired to by Korea in the twenty-first century. The Korean Classics are generally written in classical Chinese, idu (吏讀) and ancient Hangŭl, as few persons can be found fluent in classical Chinese, idu (吏讀), and English to publish studies in English. The original source texts are vast and complex, and little solid translation for the Korean Classics exists, despite the fact that many are preserved in the AKS Jangseogak (藏書閣). Archives are not difficult to find. Few agricultural scientists in Korea have given the matter much scientific thought. Yet the importance of the subject, and the difficulties involved in an official English translation, provided an irresistible charm. K-Classic series project for global communication of Korean Classics intends to provide a source of the historical context of economic development and current status of Korean economy sponsored by the Academy of Korean Studies (AKS). The series explore Agriculture, Accounting, Finance, and Business culture.

This book has been a long time in the creation; I accumulated a long list of the accountability. In 2002, I started working together with the research team which is the Global Price and Income History Group, measuring prices, incomes, and economic well-being around the world before 1950; the team is grateful for funding from the US National Science Foundation led by Lindert, Peter H.

This book also benefits greatly from the All-UC Group in Economic History and the International Institute of Social History (IISG, Netherlands, and the International Conference on Korean Studies in Souphanouvong University, Luang Prang, Lao PDR, under a leadership of Prof. Vilayphone).

During the working, a great many colleagues have helped me with queries, shared their knowledge and perspectives with me. Among those who have provided me with encouragement are Sarah Lawrence Commissioning Editor, Economics & Finance Palgrave Macmillan/Springer Nature, Prof. Daniel Jong SCHWEKENDIEK (SungKyunKwan University, Germany), Dr. James. B. Lewis (Oxford University, UK), Prof. Elisabeth Kaske (Leipzig University, Germany), Dr. Nanny Kim (Heidelberg University, Germany), Prof. Yonson Ahn (Goethe University, Germany), and Dr. Namgung Ho Sam (GangHwa County, Republic of Korea). I would like to particularly thank those students who took my classes to read all classical text and English translation, and provided me with concrete comments and reviews: Evelyn Ruiz (Republic of Peru), Paul Kim (USA), Anca Valentina (Romania), and Akhmetzianova Aisylu (Russia). I am extremely grateful to Prof. Kim Hyeon (The Academy of Korean Studies Republic of Korea), Lyndsey Twining (USA), and Sim Sanghyeon (Republic of Korea).

Ganghwa County DMZ, Korea (Republic of)   Seong Ho Jun

EXPLANATORY NOTE

The original edition of Nongsa chiksŏl (Concise Farming Talk, hereafter CFT) was printed with movable metal type and nationally dispersed to provincial officers in 1429 by the order of King Sejong. This oldest 1492 edition of CFT, composed prior to the Japanese invasions of Korea (1592–1598), is thought to be in Japan, but has not yet been found in Japan nor Korea. The English translation here is based on the editions which were Kyujanggak Royal Library preserved the 1581 edition which is King's gift to provincial governor (see Appendix A photo CFT 1 photographed by Sim Sanghyeon AKS) and the edition collected in the National Library of Korea (hereafter NLK) which is compiled in 1655 by Sin Sok as part of Nongga chipsŏng (Compilation for Farming House, hereafter CFH) which contained three books CFT (1429), Kumyang chapnok (Miscellanies on Kŭmyang District hereafter MKD), and Sasi ch'anyoch'o (Compiled Essential Excerpts on the Four Seasons hereafter CEF) (see Appendix A photo CFT 2 photographed by Sim Sanghyeon AKS).

Contents

Part I General Introduction

1 Old Wealth Horse to New Wealth Ox 3

2 Choson's Settled Population by King's Reign (1392–1910) 25

3 What Climatic Change During the First Global Age Tells Us 39

4 Emerging Seed Science in CFT 43

5 Drought: Enduring and Leguminous Plants Science 55

6 The Organization of CFT 67

7 Conclusion 73

Part II English Translation of Concise Farming Talk (Nongsa chiksŏl)

8 Preface 79

9	Preparing the Seeds	81
10	Plowing the Soil	83
11	Cultivating Hemp	85
12	Cultivating Rice	87
13	Cultivating Proso/Foxtail Millet	97
14	Cultivating Barnyard Grass	101
15	Cultivating Soybeans, Red Beans, and Mung Beans	103
16	Cultivating Barley and Wheat	105
17	Cultivating Sesame	107
18	Cultivating Buckwheat	109
19	Cultivating Cotton	111

Appendix A: Original Text of CFT and Photos CFT 1 Kyujanggak Royal Library the 1581 Edition and CFT 2 the National Library of Korea 1655 Edition — 113

Appendix B: Farming Tools in CFT and Examples in Other Sources — 175

Appendix C: Geographical Appendix of the Veritable Records of King Sejong (世宗實錄地理志) GAVK — 185

Appendix D: Glossary — 201

References — 205

Index — 211

ABBREVIATIONS

AGRICULTURE CLASSICS OF CHOSŎN REPEATEDLY CITED IN THE TEXT HAVE BEEN ABBREVIATED ACCORDING TO THE LIST BELOW:

CEF   *Compiled Essential Excerpts on the Four Seasons* (Sasi ch'anyoch'o 四時纂要抄)
CFH   *Compilation for Farming House* (Nongga chipsŏng 農家集成)
CFT   *Concise Farming Talk* (Nongsa chiksŏl 農事直說)
GAVK *Geographical Appendix of the Veritable Records of King Sejong* (世宗實錄地理志)
HDN   *Haedong nongsŏ* (海東農書, 1799)
HJN   *Hanjŏngnok* (閑情錄, 1618)
MKD   *Miscellanies on Kŭmyang District* (Kumyang chapnok 衿陽雜錄, 1492)
RASLK *Revised and Augmented Sallim kyŏngje* (增補山林經濟)
SLK   *Sallim kyŏngje* (山林經濟, 1715)

LIST OF FIGURES

Fig. 2.1	Chosŏn population by King's reign (1392–1910) (unit: thousand. *Source* Estimated data is from Kwŏn T'ae-hwan and Sin Yong-ha, "Chosŏn wangjo sidae in'gu ch'ujong e kwan han il siron," Tong'a munhwa 14 [1977.12]: 289–330)	27
Fig. 2.2	Average annual rates of population growth: Korea China and Europe ca 1400–1910 (*Source* McEvedy and Jones, *Europe and China: Atlas of World Population History* [Middlesex: Penguin Books, 1978] 18, 171, William Lavely and R. Bin Wong Revising)	27
Fig. 2.3	Korean adult male population in fifteenth century (*Source* GAVK. Legend: **A**=Seoul [109,372]; **B**=Chongsŏng [21,815]; **C**=Gilchu [14,819]; **D**=P'yŏngyang [14,440]; **E**=Kongchu [10,049])	28
Fig. 2.4	Total population in eighteenth-century Korea (Source: *Hoguchongsu*, 1789. Legend: **A**=Seoul [189,153]; **B**=P'yŏngyang [107,592]; **C**=Ŭchu [89,970]; **D**=Ch'ungchu [87,331]; **E**=Chŏnchu [72,505]; **X**=Ganggyŏ [60,419])	28
Fig. 2.5	Arable land—ratio of dry fields and wet fields in the fifteenth century (Legend: **Dark**=Wet, **Bright**=Dry)	31
Fig. 2.6	Arable Land—ratio of dry fields and wet fields in the eighteenth century (Legend: **Dark**=Wet, **Bright**=Dry)	32
Fig. 2.7	Ruralization Korea vs Urbanization UK (1392–1910)	36

Fig. 2.8 Real land value vs population (1550–1910) (*Source* Jun Seong Ho, "Wages, Rents, and Interest Rates in Southern Korea, 1700 to 1900," *Research in Economic History*, Vol. 24. Presented in WEHC Helsinki 2006, Session 21, 52)   37

Fig. 3.1 Total frequency of national disasters divided by King's reigning days   40

Fig. 5.1 Number of irrigation facilities in southern area (1470–1900) (*Source* Miyajima Hiroshi [1980] and S. H. Jun [1998])   63

List of Tables

Table 1.1	High open society Koryŏ (918–1392)	8
Table 1.2	Populations of the world's largest cities (1080–1800) (unit thousand)	13
Table 1.3	Price of rice prior to publication of CFT	18
Table 1.4	Transition of economic system in Korean historiography (918–1910)	22
Table 2.1	10 high rank of household, population, and taxable land	30
Table 5.1	Rainfall in Chosŏn (1771–1834) (unit: mm)	63
Table 5.2	Classification Standard of Rainfall for Table 5.1	65
Table C.1	Triple types of information: Household, Adult male population, Arable land unit 結 (Myŏck)	186

PART I

General Introduction

CHAPTER 1

Old Wealth Horse to New Wealth Ox

International organizations such as the Food and Agriculture Organization of the United Nation (FAO) respect techniques for managing a specific agricultural system and landscape adapted to the local environment. These are defined as "remarkable land use systems and landscapes which are rich in globally significant biological diversity evolving from the co-adaptation of a community with its environment and its needs and aspirations for sustainable development." Such useful knowledge is sought after by people across the globe today.

There is an unbelievable story for the remarkable land-use system from the Central Asia, which is Koreans became the first people who led to grow rice along the nomadic steppes, despite the local opinion that its cultivation would be impossible because of severe salt accumulation and climatic condition. In 1937, the first large-scale operation of massive deportation occurred in the Soviet under Stalin regime, about 175,000 "Koryo Saram" were relocated by brutal force from Far East to Central Asia, but their farming knowledges were so powerful that they have a world record for rice yield.[1]

The achievement of "Koryo Saram" after the Second World War was crucial to the changes in the Russian attitude toward Central Asia's economic future. In contrast to the pre-war and Cold War attitude, "Koryo Saram" was expected to use their political and economic strength to

---

[1] German Kim (2001, pp. 27–28; 2009, p. 17).

counter capitalist penetration. This change allowed "Koryo Saram" to pursue the systematic introduction of entrepreneurship to the socialistic economy.

This book is a story showing the argument and attempts to place the "Korean miracle" in the context of global history, which has the longest contextual history of a land-use system and the most significant biological diversity. The longevity and the stability of the Agrarian State have long captured the mind of the East Asia. Confucianism is an agrarianist philosophy which has been developed in the framework of the prevalent East Asian rural society of the time. It inspired global comparison with the Christian and Islamic worlds in an attempt to explain its development and survival for over millennia.

There is a comparatively unexplored question of the "Korean miracle" here, that is, how Korea managed to escape Malthusian traps and record such a vast increasing rate of population without serious worsening in the standard of living. Essentially, the same observation can be seen with regard to developments in China and Japan in the seventeenth century, which, as will be argued below, took place under the influence of the Confucian-oriented international economy of East Asia.[2]

This book shows the argument and endeavors to place the "Korean miracle" in the context of global history. It will be argued that Industrious Revolution of the East Asian multiplicity, the pillar of the stability of the world economy between 1400 and 1850, created the nomadic society-settled society harmony and succeeded to make a sustainable growth in the balanced way, emphasizing a more efficient utilization of human resources through labor-intensive farming technology.

During the last decades, there has been a discussion on the origins of the divergence between the urban economies of Europe and the lowland delta economies of East Asia. The global comparison suggests an assumption about the causes of the great divergence, linked to the different agricultural productivity which characterized the quick increase in East Asia's population since the eleventh century, while the growth of Western Europe's population did not occur until the late eighteenth century.

Keeping in mind Thomas Malthus' theory, it may be difficult to maintain the same longevity of agricultural fertility for a dense population in

[2] T. Giovanni Arrighi (2004, Chapter 3, p. 81).

Europe as was achieved in East Asia. Western Europe escaped from a constant population in the late eighteenth century, so-called Malthusian trap, thanks to Industrial Revolution. On the other hand, East Asia did enjoy the longevity of high productivity of agriculture.

However, the biggest challenge for East Asian's economic historians is to explain the differences in wealth between sedentary life based on the lowland s of southwest and pastoral life on the upland of northeast occurred concurrently with the Agriculture Revolution. The discussions around the great divergence between Europe and Asia have attempted to overcome a Eurocentric bias through reference to global comparisons and connections. However, these comparisons fall into a "Sino-centric bias," so-called Sino-barbarian frame, because they only consider the lowland Yangzi Delta and some parts of Japan and India, while completely overlooking Korea and Northeast Asia.

This "Sino-centric bias" is caused by twofold lineages of empires experiencing difficulties in achieving cultural fusion. One lineage includes Tang (618–906), Song (960–1270), and Ming (1368–1644), who continued to pursue the stability of sedentary life in the lowlands, especially the delta areas. The other includes the empires Koguyŏ (37 BCE–668), the Khitan/Liao (916–1125), the Jurchen/Jin (1115–1234), Yuan (1279–1368), and Qing (1644–1911), who had always practiced their time-honored pastoral life in upland area.

The mystery of whether the origin of East Asian agricultural techniques is in the upland, mountainous districts or lowland delta areas cannot be known for certain. However, it is a common consensus that for the greater part of the past millennium the food situation was considerably better in the lowland delta than in the uplands. For this reason, East Asia's lowland populations were able to increase quickly since the eleventh century, while a rapid population growth in the uplands still awaits today.

CFT tells a different story from the common sense that was the heart of the early-modern Korean Agricultural Revolution. Natural resources, the rainfall of Korean Peninsula and particularly Northeast Asia, were always a limitation for rice cultivation, and to overcome such a limitation, there was a need to develop techniques for a drought-resistant cropping system. The CFT introduces a drought-resistant cropping system based on dry fields, which allowed Korean farmers to extend the agricultural frontier, especially for rice, from the upland, well-watered mountainous area to the lowlands, deltas, and basins.

This book brings attention to the transition of the Korean economy's center of gravity from upland to lowland. The transition happened during one century of an unusually tyrannical government and a long series of natural calamities during the same period as the Black Death, which seems to have disappeared into a kind of black hole in general East Asian studies.

As many East Asian specialists have already pointed out, it is too difficult to find a dynamic transition for the economic history of East Asia. However, by taking Korean historiography, we can try to illuminate the dark Sino-centric bias which has concealed the regional diversity and global interdependence of pre-modern East Asia. This "Sino-centric bias" is caused by twofold lineages of empires experiencing difficulties in achieving cultural fusion. One lineage includes Tang (618–906), Song (960–1270), and Ming (1368–1644), who exclusively stood China, regarded themselves as the most prominent civilization in the world that had gained the Mandate of Heaven. The other includes the empires Koguyŏ (37 BCE–668), the Khitan/Liao (916–1125), the Jurchen/Jin (1115–1234), Yuan (1279–1368), and Qing (1644–1911), who were regarded as the only legitimate Emperor of the entire world under Heaven had always practiced their time-honored pastoral life in upland area. Owing to it, few people are aware that there was a real relationship between Koryŏ (918–1392) and the Jurchen Jin, which was reestablished in late Chosŏn (post-1634) and Qing.

In the late nineteenth century, Koreans were the first people who began to grow rice along the nomadic steppes, despite the local opinion that its cultivation would be impossible. They were also the first to begin to cultivate green bristle grass and beans in the region. Their successes were so powerful that they have found reflection in the governmental documents of the time.[3]

Thus, the task of this book is to readdress the period from 918 to 1550 as an integral part of East Asian economic history. In the end, Koryŏ and Chosŏn are required to figure out the solution of the puzzle that plays an essential role in the platform of cultural fusion between the sedentary and the nomad.

We can find a clue of the puzzle from the name of Korea and Chosŏn. The name "Korea" was not confined to Korean Peninsula. It might have

[3] Valeriy S. Khan (2011, pp. 4–5).

first appeared in the Western world through Marco Polo (1254–1324). In 1933, an artifact appeared in the Reports of the Librarian of Congress of the USA connected with Marco Polo's secret map where he mentioned Korea as Cauly and Kauli. In modern Korea, Cauly is pronounced as "Kuri," transcribed with various Chinese characters, but the phonetic meaning indicates bronze yellow. The modern name "Korea" is derived from the name Koryŏ, which itself has its origin in the name Koguryŏ, which signifies the iconic supremacy of the horse archer. They were the highest expert archers; skilled horse-riding archers used cavalry as their main force in hunting.[4]

The map has several interesting things that are important for the economic history of Korea. The first is the international trade in regard to the spaces of Tartar and Kuril on the map, approximately covering today's North Korean territory with Russia. Marco Polo met there a merchant from Syria dealing Korean tiger furs, which means inter-continental trade already existed in northeastern region. These are very important historical facts for cultural fusion. There are many records that the Jurchen Jin and Khitan Liao traded with furs, skins, horses, silver, and gold from the tenth century onward, at least according to the historical records from Korea. The growth of international trade between the Islamic world and Buddhist world was never accompanied by imperialism, which tended to make equality, particularly among steppe, desert, and tropical zones (see Tables 1.1, 1.2).

The second is the numeral code recorded on the map as the copyist recorded it. It is the numeral system used by the merchants of Kaesŏng City (the capital of Koryŏ, located just north of the DMZ in present-day North Korea) from the eleventh century. These merchants have been famous for their commercial acumen and bookkeeping methods, which seem to have changed little over time.

People always confused the correlation among Cathay, Djerdja (Jurchen), Kŏlhan (Ch'i-tan), and Chosŏn; the word Kŏlhan (Ch'i-tan, Cathay) still appeared occasionally in European writings. Even today, in Russia, Greece, Persia, and Turkestan, "Khitay" in its different variants has remained the general designation for China. Middle East historians extended the name Cathay to Djerdja (Jurchen), when Koryŏ had the great triumph after destruction of Liao and Djerdja (Jurchen) defeated Song. But it is very clear when we read *"The Liao Shih, in the Standard*

[4] Jing-shen Tao (1976, p. 9).

8 S. H. JUN

Table 1.1 High open society Koryŏ (918–1392)

Year	Song (total) Visiting for trade from 明州/福州	Song/Quanzhou (泉州, 福建) Visiting for trade from 明州/福州	Song Visiting for trade from 明州/登州/廣州/上海	Song Visiting for trade from 廣州	Song Naturalized people (immigration)	Khitan/Liao Visiting for trade	Khitan/Liao Naturalized people (immigration)	Balhae Naturalized people (immigration)	Manchu/Jurchen/Jin Visiting for trade	Manchu/Jurchen/Jin Naturalized people (immigration)	Japan Visiting for trade	Japan Naturalized people (immigration)	Tamra Visiting for trade	Saracen
921'														
941'									1					
942'														
948'									1					
999'									20			20		
1005'						1						35		
1012'			1		1					370				
1013'					10									
1015'					1									
1016'					1		119							
1017'	40	40					104							
1018'	200	200					10		20					
1019'	1								102					
1020'		1								261				
1021'	1													
1022'		1							30					
1024'														100

1 OLD WEALTH HORSE TO NEW WEALTH OX

Year									
1025'									100
1027'									
1028'	30	30							
1029'	80	1	80						
1030'	1								
1031'						200	300		
1032'				506		130	27		
1033'	55	55		59		110	340		
1034'				121	52	389			
1035'			12	29	39	219	6		
1036'	67	67				513			
1037'	1	1				272			
1038'	147	147				351			
1039'	50	50				877			
1040'	1	1		40		59		26	
1041'						187			
1042'						738	14		
1043'						229			
1044'						290			
1045'		1				343			
1046'						446			
1047'									
1048'	133	133				199	342		
1049'						248			
1050'						91			
1051'	101	101				57			
1052'						96	48		
1053'	69	69				63			
1054'						85			
1055'				15		53			
1056'	29	29				100		1	
1057'	58	58				50			

(continued)

Table 1.1 (continued)

Year	Song (total) Visiting for trade from 明州/温州	Song/Quanzhou (明州, 泉州) Visiting for trade from 明州/温州	Song Visiting for trade from 明州/温州/密州/上海	Song Visiting for trade from 高麗	Song Naturalized people (immigration)	Khitan/Liao Visiting for trade	Khitan/Liao Naturalized people (immigration)	Balhae Naturalized people (immigration)	Manchu/Jurchen/Jin Visiting for trade	Manchu/Jurchen/Jin Naturalized people (immigration)	Japan Visiting for trade	Japan Naturalized people (immigration)	Tamra Visiting for trade	Saracen
1058'	1	1							57					
1059'	1	1							123					
1060'	124	124							46					
1061'	1	1												
1062'									6					
1063'	2	2							2					
1064'	2	2					2							
1065'	2	2							66					
1066'														
1067'														
1068'	2	2												
1069'	2	2					8							
1070'	1	1							69					
1071'	150	150							2					
1072'	1	1								25	75			
1073'										1238	39			
1074'	8	8		8					38					

1 OLD WEALTH HORSE TO NEW WEALTH OX   11

Year							
1075'	74		74				
1076'							
1077'	77	2	77		49		
1078'	2	1	2		78		
1079'	107		107		23	14	
1080'	2	1	2		27		
1081'	98		98			17	1
1082'	1		1		8		1
1083'					1		
1084'					20		1
1085'							
1086'							
1087'	40		40		51		72
1088'							1
1089'	226		226		21		
1090'	150		150		88		
1091'					40		
1092'					41		
1093'	3		3				
1094'	134	1	134		76		194
1095'	31		31		196		80
1096'	30		30		105		
1097'	36		36		3		
1098'	20		20		26		
1099'					1		
1100'	2	1	2				1
1101'							
1102'					111		
1103'	45	3	45		262		
1104'	1		1		79	1753	
1105'							

(continued)

Table 1.1 (continued)

	Song (total) Visiting for trade from 密州/明州	Song/Quanzhou Visiting for trade from 密州/明州 (密州, 泉州)	Song Visiting for trade from 明州/華亭/慶源/上海	Song Visiting for trade from 慶源	Song Naturalized people (immigration)	Khitan/Liao Visiting for trade	Khitan/Liao Naturalized people (immigration)	Balhae Naturalized people (immigration)	Manchu/Jurchen/Jin Visiting for trade	Manchu/Jurchen/Jin Naturalized people (immigration)	Japan Visiting for trade	Japan Naturalized people (immigration)	Tamra Visiting for trade	Saracen
1106'									110					
1107'									25					
1108'									150					
1109'														
1110'														
1111'														
1112'														
1113'														
1114'								44						
1115'							275							
1116'										3230				
1117'										1863				
1118'														
1119'														

Table 1.2 Populations of the world's largest cities (1080–1800) (unit thousand)

Place		Year				
		1080–1232	1500	1600	1700	1800
Korea	Kaesŏng	500–1000ª				
	Hansŏng (Seoul)		103	95	185	204
China	Quanzhou (泉州)	225–1000				
Italy	Naples		150	281	216	427
	Venice		100	139	138	138
	Milan		100	120	124	135
France	Paris		100	220	510	581
	Amsterdam		14	65	200	217
England	London		40	200	575	865
Iraq	Baghdad	300				

Sources Koryŏsa chŏlyo 1232. 6. KRSC 16:15a. Clark, *Community, Trade, and Networks* (1991): 76; Maddison, *The World Economy* (2001): 54; McEvedy and Jones, *Atlas of World Population History* (1978): 171; Kwŏn and Shin, "Chosŏn wangjo" (1977.12): 289–330
ªThe population originally was recorded as 100,000 households, which can be calculated as approximately 500,000 people: 崔瑀 議遷都時 國家昇平旣久 京都戶至十萬. KRSC 16:15a. but Japanese survey reported the population of Kaesŏng was 1,000,000 people. 朝鮮總督府, 調査資料第十一輯, 1925, p. 11

History of the Liao Dynasty" which introduces the name Chosŏn first as Kŏlhan (Ch'i-tan, Cathay) phonetically meaning Great Han. The name of Chosŏn also was not confined to Korean Peninsula. Chosŏn is the tribal ancestor of Cathay, is phonetically same name with Djerdja (Jurchen), and is also related to Chorcha and Churchin which is listed on *The Travels of Marco Polo*.[5]

From the eleventh to the fourteenth centuries, Koryŏ Korea was a leader in a medieval economic revolution with the Song, the Khitan Liao, the Jurchen Jin, and Yuan who continued to pursue harmony between the sedentary life and nomadic life. The Northern Song (960–1127) and the Southern Song (1127–1279) were an economic giant in the delta area and sea but military weaker in the upland, steppe, deserts, and plains.

During the medieval economic revolution, there were many seaport cities in the Yellow Sea region; for example, Dengzhou, Hangzhou, Mingzhou, Yangzhou, Quanzhou, Guangzhou, and Kaesŏng left behind a great cultural legacy as international centers of trade, but their life for

---

[5] Marco Polo (1993, p. 231).

gateway was too short to play a role in soft power engine of maritime economy except Kaesŏng, which was unique gateway city permanently opening for the period. The sea vessels in Kaesong were crowded per day around one thousand, but the countpartner for Kaesŏng from Song was openly closed and moved to other places because of the conflict between Song and Ch'i-tan Liao, Jurchen Jin and Mongol. That is a main reason why the cities of Kaesŏng and Koryŏ society and economy were known to have trading prowess, which led to mercantilism and something of a commercial revolution. During the early Chosŏn period (pre-1592), some residual effects of Koryŏ society were still detectable. But the late Chosŏn was marked by a quite different growth trajectory along the lines of Smithian physiocracy.

According to Angus Maddison, East Asia (China, Korea, and Japan) constituted the largest economic region in 1820, producing more than one-third of the world's total production.[6] Although it went into a decline in the late Chosŏn period as compared to the Koryŏ period, Kaesŏng's importance in the Koryŏ economy and its reservoir of commercial talent during Chosŏn cannot be underestimated.

We know from descriptions that from the eleventh to the thirteenth centuries, the city of Kaesŏng was one of the trading epicenters of the world. From the late tenth century, Koryŏ triumphed over northern rivals and strengthened its southern bases, opening them for international trade.

Until the tenth century, Koryŏ's international trade was conducted through the port of Kaesŏng linked to the port of Dengzhou in Song China, but after Koryŏ was defeated, Khitan trade from Kaesŏng shifted to Quanzhou. Even though Koryŏ cut off all diplomatic relations with Song in 996, the trade continued throughout the eleventh century supported by periodic issues of bronze coins minted by both Koryŏ and Song.

The population of Kaesŏng grew during Koryŏ's prosperous times (1020–1230), and it became linked with Quanzhou. From the eleventh to the thirteenth centuries, Koryŏ was a strong international trading power in East Asia. That was a period when movable metal type, ginseng, Korean paper, Confucian education, and the Koreana Tripitaka were all developed and traded, and commercialization and urbanization reached unprecedented heights in East Asia. Trade with the north and trade with China were completely different and had diverse purposes. Important trading items with Song China were Neo-Confucian books

[6]Angus Maddison (2007, Appendix A).

and Buddhist scriptures, which enabled cultural connections with Song that could promote diplomatic bargaining against northern regions. During that period of peace, trade was used to promote Koryŏ's sovereignty and stature as a civilized state.

During Kaesŏng's heyday, most of the world's major cities were not to be found in Europe. Baghdad under the Abbasids boasted a population of 300,000 by the ninth century. Although population is difficult to determine, a Japanese survey (1925) reported that, around the eleventh century, there were one million people living in Kaesŏng. Marco Polo was overwhelmed by Quanzhou, one of Kaesŏng's trading partners, and he called it the world's largest international trading port. Koryŏ had a rich urban tradition, and Kaesŏng was one of the world's largest cities along with Quanzhou (see Table 1.2).

East Asian and Middle Eastern cities flourished, but, beginning in the fifteenth century, Western European cities, especially Italian cities, began to emerge as commercial centers, because their governments promoted commercial development, developed transportation technologies, and built infrastructure to support trade. By the time Venice, Naples, and Milan became some of the most populous in the world in the fifteenth century, the city culture of Kaesŏng and even Hanyang (Seoul) appeared economically, technologically, politically, and culturally "backward."

The Japanese invasions of the 1590s caused a radical shift to a "backward" closing-off cities from most international influence. For Chosŏn international trade from Kaesŏng was an exception, as its ginseng trade reached into China and Japan. In the late nineteenth century, Korean cities started to be affected by the new urban culture that had been developed in Western Europe and which was being enthusiastically introduced by Japan, especially to Tongnae (Pusan). Research on Korean urbanism has often asked why Kaesŏng was the exception, both before the opening of the ports and in the way modernity shaped other Korean cities after the opening of the ports. The answers have generally been unsatisfactory.

This book is an economic history of the Chosŏn dynasty (1392–1910). Chosŏn is not only known for managing the regions of northeastern part of Asia for 500 years as the exemplar of Confucianism, but was also one of the greatest so-called agricultural states under Heaven. Chosŏn has been introduced through academic exploration by Western scholars, but their findings have some limitations. The period during the first global age during 1400–1600, in particular, has been too poorly reported on in English to be brought to the attention of the Western knowledge society and was never considered by the California School of economic history.

The Chosŏn court led the establishment of an agricultural knowledge system and published many books in cooperation with seasoned farmers. Among many other government-sponsored publications, two books about agriculture, in particular, were published in fifteenth century. The first volume is CFT, the publication of which was initiated by King Sejong in 1429. The second volume is MKD written by Kang Hŭimaeng and printed by the government in 1492.

CFT reflects on these systems, resulting in the longevity and stability of outstanding landscapes, the maintenance and adoption of agricultural variability, the resiliency of ecosystems, as well as sustainable food and livelihood security for the northern part of the Korean Peninsula. However, policy during the Japanese colonial period (1910–1945) unfortunately neglected traditional systems and overlooked many parts of biological diversity. This book delves deeply into the experiences and wisdom of the seasoned farmers for the revelation of the forgotten knowledge from the Land of the Morning Calm.

This book touches that Koreans experienced a transition from the nomadic pastoral world to the settled agricultural world to maximize food production, resulting in Korea's transformation into a great so-called agricultural state under Heaven. This book not only tells Koreans transformation from the horse archer to the cultivator with plowing paired oxen, but also a platform for the fusion between the old and new world orders which is the bonded alliance between Chosŏn and Ming, two Confucian states with a main economic policy of the "physiocratic model" for small peasants.

The Korean Peninsula is mountainous and stretches mainly between 50 degrees and 30 degrees latitude, in a northeast-southwest orientation. The climate variance is extreme. The north always experiences cold, dry winters, blasted by Siberian winds, while the south has mild, wet winters and hot, humid summers drenched by the summer monsoon.

These variable conditions from northeast to southwest present great difficulties for developing the food cereal crops. Northern Korea's high altitude and steep slopes make a large part of its territory virtually unusable for agricultural purposes, with only limited possibilities, compared to the southern part of Korea.

The experience of fatal famines during the first global ages, which rampant pirates annually invaded the ricebasket of Korea (Chŏlla and

Gyŏngsang Provinces), made it difficult for a lowland-oriented development strategy, for example, a maritime-oriented opening policy for international trade. Although Chosŏn in fifteenth century already had an understanding of the Eurasian continent and its oceans, as is demonstrated by the Integrated Map of Historical Capitals (*Honil kangni yŏktae kukto chido*[7]), which includes Africa, Europe, and India, the ocean always remained too much of a high danger zone for Koreans to partake in exploration. The awareness of ocean routes was not linked to an opening up between Asia and Europe, and this was a factor for the process of divergence.

The closed maritime ports of Korea continued until Western capitalism knocked on their doors in the mid-nineteenth century. This is the main reason for the dichotomy between muted global market fluctuations compared to their impact on the urban commercialized economies of Europe.[8] When new maritime nations like Portugal and Spain encompassed the East Asia, their trading partners changed to smuggling and pirates' groups during the first global ages.

Ming China also rejected the maritime port opening policies and took the exclusively institutionalized zone of the new agronomic world order, even while marking the highest point of Chinese naval history with Zeng He's great voyages. However, despite the fact that Westerners suffered from famines as well, their dream differed fundamentally from the East. For Western explorers like Vasco da Gama, the ocean was a source of the ambition. The divergence of visions between the East and the West during the fifteenth century led to an unintegrated wave in global history. The main reason for the dichotomy is the different response to food famine.

As the concern for the food skyrocketed, the commercial power of medieval cities declined and was replaced by peasantry. Therefore, rice became the gold standard, and many paddy fields in the western part of Korea were called golden places. For example, the name of the city of Kimpo (home of Gimpo International Airport) literally means "golden port," as it was one of the highest yielding rice fields.

---

[7] 混一疆理歷代國都之圖.
[8] Jane Kate Leonard (2008, pp. 7–9).

Table 1.3 Price of rice prior to publication of CFT

	1412	1423
High quality horses (per head)	450 sheets	1350 sheets
Copper coins (per string gwan)	10 sheets	30 sheets
Rice (per mal, about 6 liters)	1 sheet	10 sheets
Cotton cloth (per bolt width about 32.80 cm, length about 16.34 meters)	30 sheets	100 sheets

Source Annals of King Sejong 05/05/21 1423, Annals of King Sejong 27/10/11 1445, Annals of King Sŏngchong 04/05/05

The opportunities and challenges of developing a peasant society in the fifteenth century led to the establishment of Confucian institutions for facilitating the growth of the fiduciary system for managing granary. Innovations for seed science led to a bilateral relationship between the two East Asian pillars—Korea and China. At the same time, expanding cultivation and ruralization further weakened the medieval urbanized commercial economy changing both the political structure and the economic structure of the East Asia (see Table 1.3; rice price rapidly increases before the publication of CFT).

The Confucian countries' alliance had gained power by keeping away Japanese pirates in a series of successful engagements. Chosŏn passionately developed agricultural knowledge and cut merchants out of international trade, enjoying a state-led monopolistic bilateral trade with Ming while especially cooperating with seed of grain and plowed oxen.

Thus, the cattle plowing has an indispensable relationship with the physiocracy of Chosŏn society. F. H. King, an American agriculturist at the end of the nineteenth century, also recorded cattle plowing as a signature characteristic of Korean farming. He says that Korean farming is characterized by mixed cropping and intercropping, mostly with soybeans, by making a narrow dam in a rice field or a paddy and plowing with two cows. His observation indicates that horses plowed in Japan while two oxen did the job in Korea. He left the following remark:

> Here in Japan the plowing was being done mostly with horses instead of the heavy bullocks so exclusively employed in Korea. Coming from China into Korea, and from there into Japan, it appeared very clear that in agricultural methods and appliances the Koreans and Japanese are more closely similar than the Chinese and Koreans, and the more we came to see off the Japanese methods the more strongly the impression became fixed that

the Japanese had derived their methods either from the Koreans or the Koreans had taken theirs more largely from Japan than from China.[9]

To illustrate just how important cattle were, Chosŏn implemented a policy of forbidding beef consumption that strictly prohibited the slaughter of cattle outside from butcher house, which was the only place which allowed the slaughtering. This policy, which continued until the late Chosŏn dynasty, was institutionalized in 1420. In CFT, it was not only the seasoned farmer but also the ox that did the great labor. The power of an ox in the fifteenth century was a force that replaced that of nine farmers' labor. The most impressive thing for the author of *Farmers of Forty Centuries* on a train trip to Kyushu from Korea was the plowing oxen, featured in CFT. While oxen were used for plowing in Korea at that time, horses were used for the same job in Japan. Plowing with cows was the most important element for production in the tillage techniques of CFT.

This technology requires highly skilled technicians as in today's operation of heavy equipment, a farmer tilling with his cow required just as much skill as a modern worker with his forklift. Among the famous Korean genre-painter Kim Hong-do's eighteenth-century works, there is a picture of plowing with paired oxen.[10]

A Confucian disciple emphasized the importance of the cow to national management in the period of Sejong and described the relationship among CFT, cows, and Sejong as follows:

> Because the laypersons only pursue their interests and do not know righteousness, they whip and scold cows when making them work, and eat them without any hesitation. Then, when the horns are crooked and the hoofs worn out, they slaughter them without pity. If a generous person or a gentleman sees it, he will have pity on the animal and is willing to think about how to correct it. This is why our King Sejong enlightened his people with regard to the cows by addressing them in *Nongsa chiksŏl* that he published and disseminated. Alas, although the heart of the great king who loves his people and creatures is enough to reform the minds to the ends of the world and restore virtuous customs, it is lamentable that his words have ended up as mere empty letters on the paper.[11]

---

[9] F. H. King (1911, p. 101).
[10] 金弘道: 1745–1806.
[11] 尹愭: 1741–1826.

As he emphasized, the cows were the important production element in the national policy of the Chosŏn dynasty, which adopted physiocracy as its governing principle. The importance of cows can also be seen through the *Royal Ancestral Rite for the God of Agriculture*, which was one of the five national rituals. This ritual, led by the king, was one of the annual national events prepared by the Ministry of Rites. The specific date of the event was determined by the Bureau of Astronomy on an auspicious day chosen among days leading up to Kyŏngch'ip (approximately March 5–6). The Ministry of Rites prepared the various kinds of farm equipment and the cattle needed for plowing and then performed the ritual on a scale as magnificent as the military inspection of troops. The highlight of the ceremony was plowing a field by driving a well-trained ox.

The importance of plowing ox as a production factor, as covered in CFT, can be seen in the existence of a husbandry-specific veterinary book published in the Sejong era. The book was published in 1430, the year following the publication of CFT. After completing the compilation of CFT in 1429 and disseminating it across the country in 1430, King Sejong commanded his subjects to investigate and report on technical books to treat livestock diseases. One such book was *Medical Prescriptions for Cattle and Horses*.[12]

In this way, King Sejong committed himself to protecting the plowing oxen from the beginning of his reign. However, in 1431, when he compiled and spread it to the whole country, he was informed that the Chinese envoy would be coming with the emperor's letter to trade ten thousand cows. He then discussed it with the major ministers such as Hwang Hŭi[13] and Maeng Sasŏng.[14] Their assistance at that time was noteworthy: While King Sejong said that he had to leave this job to Yun Pong, the person in charge of the northern region at that time, to solve it diplomatically, Hwang Hŭi suggested that he select a person with a high command of Chinese and make him report the situation of how negotiations went in the residence of the envoy.[15]

---

[12] Annals of King Sejong, 12/03/18 1430.
[13] 黃喜: 1363–1452.
[14] 孟思誠: 1360–1438.
[15] Annals of King Sejong, 13/12/05 1431.

On December 13, a party with the Chinese envoy was held at the T'aep'yŏnggwan to resolve diplomatic issues. Adopting a very modest posture, Sejong stressed that in Chosŏn, with scarce resources, it was hard for his people to make ends meet due to the recurrent floods and droughts, and that plowing cows were a very important resource for the country. Sejong asked the envoy to report to his emperor that Chosŏn could not afford to his request for the trade of ten thousand cows. Upon hearing this, ChāngShèng, the Chinese envoy, made a pledge that he would obtain an exception as he himself did before when addressing the trade of values such of gold and silver.

The Chosŏn dynasty's policy of respecting plowing ox was not only a basic domestic policy but also a policy that served to calm and stabilize external diplomacy and counteract the northern people's turbulence. It was a policy that provided Chosŏn with plowing oxen by calming the militant and aggressive people living in the northern regions of the country. In the implementation of this policy, it was very important to efficiently raise cattle in stables and to utilize them in producing a natural source of fertilizer and for plowing rather than just using them as meat. Especially in the time of King Sejong, the policy was a very important one that incorporated agriculture into foreign affairs policy. Immediately after the compilation of CFT, King Sejong provided the people living in the northern region of Chosŏn with plowing cows, food, and clothing to make them concentrate on farming and turn away from their more warlike tendencies.[16]

In the meanwhile, the Ming government had a high demand for military horses for its campaigns against the northern Mongol. The Chosŏn enjoyed interlinked trade between the Jurchen and the Ming in the late fourteenth and early fifteenth centuries. In fact, it has been shown that paper money issuance was based on funds which had originated from military horse trade with Ming. From 1401 to 1411, Ming requested 10,000 horses. In 1411, 30,000 bolts of silk and 20,000 bolts of cotton were paid for 10,000 horses.[17] The domestic price for these horses in Korea was only 14,000 bolts of silk, leaving a government profit of

---

[16] Annals of King Sejong, 13/12/13 1431.
[17] Annals of King Taejong, 11/01/20 1411.

Table 1.4 Transition of economic system in Korean historiography (918–1910)

Dynasty	Key currency	Supplementary currency	Soft power plant	Main industry	Space for market	Golden ages
Koryŏ (918–1392)	Vase shaped silver coins	Bronze coin/iron coin hemp clothes	Buddhism temple	International big business for luxury goods	Urban city	996–1271
Chosŏn (1392–1910)	Copper coins	Rice/cotton clothes/ iron currency in the shape of an arrowhead/paper note	Confucianism academy	Domestic small business	Rural town	1418–1545, 1675–1799

Source Jun Seong Ho, Monetary authority independence and stability in medieval Korea: The Koryŏ monetary system through four centuries of East Asian transformations, 918–1392. *Financial History Review*, Vol. 21, No. 03, pp. 259–280, December 2014

16,000 bolts, which were used as backing for the issue of paper money (see Table 1.3).

To benefit from the state monopoly of foreign trade and the innovation of mining techniques, the sovereignty of the monetary system took decisive action to issue paper money. At first, paper money was issued, but copper coins soon followed.[18] Because Ming China was particularly interested in Korean horses, most transactions with China were carried out in gold and silver used occasionally in interstate trade. Gradually, gold and silver acquired in the horse trade circulated within the Korean Peninsula, although conflicts with the Mongols at times interrupted trade during the early years of the Ming. With the trade keeping the balance in the black with Ming, the Chosŏn dynasty tried to transform the basic system from commercial life combined with urban life into agriculturally settled habitation in rural areas.

Furthermore, they shifted the center of knowledge production from the Buddhist temple to the Confucian academy, which made a great fiduciary power for the management of the granary. International trade networks based on Buddhism were destroyed as never before, but their legacy changed into a writing power for the state's internal control system of the authoritative sanction for intended fraud and unintended error. However, the question remains: Why was it the anti-Buddhist Confucian Reformation which contributed to changes in agricultural productivity. The Confucian ethic fostered industrious hard work,

[18] Peng Xinwei (1994, p. 471).

competing thinking for efficiency of farming, division of family labor, and "Smithian Physiocratic virtues" which facilitated neutrality of money in the market (Table 1.4).

REFERENCES

Angus Maddison. *The World Economy: A Millennial Perspective*. Paris: Development Centre of the Organisation for Economic Co-operation and Development, 2007.
F. H. King. *Farmers of Forty Centuries, or Permanent Agriculture in China, Korea and Japan*. Madison, 1911.
German Kim. *Ethnic Enterpreneurship of Koreans in the USSR and Post Soviet and Central Asia* (No. 445). Institute of Developing Economies Japan External Trade Organization, 2009.
German Kim. Koryo Saram: Koreans in the Former. *USSR Korean and Korean American Studies Bulletin*, Vol. 12, Nos. 2/3, 2001.
Jane Kate Leonard. *Metals, Monies, and Markets in Early Modern Societies: East Asian and Global Perspectives*. Monies, Market, and Finance in China and East Asia, Vol. 1. BUNKA - WENHUA. Tubinger Ostasiatische Forschungen. Tuebingen East Asian Studies (17), 2008.
Jing-shen Tao. *The Jurchen in Twelfth-Century China: A Study of Sinicization*. Seattle: University of Washington Press, 1976.
Jun Seong Ho. Monetary Authority Independence and Stability in Medieval Korea: The Koryŏ Monetary System Through Four Centuries of East Asian Transformations, 918–1392. *Financial History Review*, Vol. 21, No. 3, pp. 259–280, December 2014.
The Travels of Marco Polo. The Complete Yule-Cordier Edition. New York: Dover Book 1, 2 Publications, 1993.
Peng Xinwei. *A Monetary History of China*, Vol. 2. Translated by Edward H. Kaplan. Western Washington University, 1994.
T. Giovanni Arrighi, Takeshi Hamashita, and Mark Selden, eds. *The Resurgence of East Asia 500, 150 and 50 Year Perspectives*. London: RoutledgeCurzon, 2004.
Valeriy S. Khan. The Contributions of Koreans to the Socio-Economic Development and Culture of Central Asia, 3rd World Congress of Korean Studies, History Session 4, The Academy of Korean Studies Seoul, 2011.

CHAPTER 2

Chosŏn's Settled Population by King's Reign (1392–1910)

The upland mountainous area of Northeast Asia and well-watered hilly places were the cradle of Korean civilization. In ancient Northeast Asia, rice was a less important crop than bean, barley, millet, wheat, buckwheat, and hemp, which were mostly cultivated in dry fields and indigenous to Northeast Asia. From the standpoint of the history of land utilization and the cropping system, the minority of wet field farming in the low land and the high frequency of references to dry field and early-sowing varieties up to the fifteenth century are not to be questioned.

In view of the cultural blending of Chosŏn economic history, it is not astonishing that data on population in early Chosŏn (pre-1592) are in the main related to three types of information: per household organized by agricultural output unit of 8 *myŏck*,[1] only adult male account for the population unit *chŏng*,[2] and arable land measured by output unit *myŏck, chim, mukŭm, zŭm*.[3] These special terms are written in *Idu*, literally meaning official's reading, which is an ancient writing system that denotes the Korean language and Korean phonology through Chinese characters. The system was first developed in Koguyŏ.[4]

---

[1] 8 *Myŏck* (結) = 1 *chubi* (注比).
[2] *Chŏng* (丁) includes males over 15 years old.
[3] 100 *chim* (卜) = 1 *myŏck* (結), 10 *mukkŭm* (束) = *chim* (卜), 10 Zŭm (把) = 1 mukkŭm (束).
[4] Peter Lee (2003, p. 27).

© The Author(s) 2019
S. H. Jun, *Agriculture and Korean Economic History*,
https://doi.org/10.1007/978-981-32-9319-9_2

The conditions of the population, tax, and land size of Chosŏn period are stimulated by the overall amalgamations. Amalgamation is a long tradition in the central nomad region. Nevertheless, they add considerably to a thoughtfulness of the physiocracy organization during the period to which they refer.[5] The estimate of the population of early Chosŏn has been based on these triple series of figures. These types became fused through economic and cultural differences: The population data focusing on adult male are nomadic, while the household and arable land are sedentary. This is why numerical estimate of the population in early Chosŏn is not easy.

Nonetheless, Chosŏn's data on population are rich. The data are either dated or clearly defined through the creation of serial databases, can show us trends with market information in food prices, non-food prices, and land prices for the Chosŏn period. When these are compared to trends in population, rainfall, disease, and a number of variables with the Western world, we can begin to rethink Malthus's talk for Chosŏn Korea. This book accounts for all those conditions which have made it conceivable for such dense populations to be sustained so largely upon the harvests of Korean soils.

Looking retrospectively, until the fifteenth century, the Djerdja (Jurchen) and Kŏlhan (Ch'i-tan, Cathay) migrated en masse to the northern part of Korea. The continual development of this vast upland area gradually brought about an Agriculture Revolution in the economic geography of Korea. By the sixteenth century, the upland had become Chosŏn's economic center of gravity and the granary of the country.

Yet the peak population and household registered in the fifteenth century by province were mostly located in upland Hamgyŏng and P'yŏngan Provinces as compared with the southern part of Korea. Even if the data are considerably below the truth, owing to omissions and evasions, it is likely that only certain parts of the upland area were relatively fully developed in the sedentary sense.

If we look at Figs. 2.1 and 2.2, the growth rate in Korea from 1400 to 1500 takes up the highest position in the world. The rising trend continued for one hundred years. Europe and even China never reached such high population growth as in Korea. This means Korean soil was used to produce sufficiently for the maintenance of high rates. In the

---

[5] Karl A. Wittfogel (1946, pp. 52–58).

2 CHOSŎN'S SETTLED POPULATION BY KING'S REIGN (1392–1910)   27

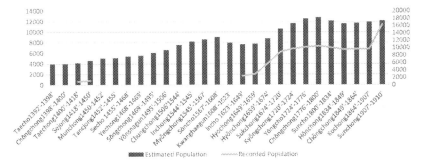

Fig. 2.1 Chosŏn population by King's reign (1392–1910) (unit: thousand. *Source* Estimated data is from Kwŏn T'ae-hwan and Sin Yong-ha, "Chosŏn wangjo sidae in'gu ch'ujong e kwan han il siron," Tong'a munhwa 14 [1977.12]: 289–330)

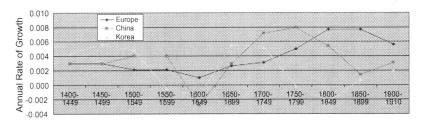

Fig. 2.2 Average annual rates of population growth: Korea China and Europe ca 1400–1910 (*Source* McEvedy and Jones, *Europe and China: Atlas of World Population History* [Middlesex: Penguin Books, 1978] 18, 171, William Lavely and R. Bin Wong Revising)

case of Korea's fifteenth-century expansion, the interaction of population with producible input such as efficient land use needs to be considered. The nonstop expansion until eighteenth century, with the exception of the period aroused Japanese invasion (1592–1598), contrasts with European countries.

From the fifteenth to seventeenth centuries, the average annual rates of population growth in East Asia roughly show synchronization until the mid-eighteenth century, but the graph tells us that from the mid-eighteenth century, Korea, China, and Europe experienced a great divergence, even though what occurred around the time of the Japanese invasions

Fig. 2.3 Korean adult male population in fifteenth century (*Source* GAVK. Legend: A = Seoul [109,372]; B = Chongsŏng [21,815]; C = Gilchu [14,819]; D = P'yŏngyang [14,440]; E = Kongchu [10,049])

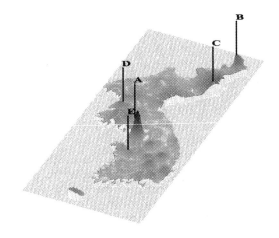

Fig. 2.4 Total population in eighteenth-century Korea (Source: *Hoguchongsu*, 1789. Legend: A = Seoul [189,153]; B = P'yŏngyang [107,592]; C = Ŭchu [89,970]; D = Ch'ungchu [87,331]; E = Chŏnchu [72,505]; X = Ganggyŏ [60,419])

(1592–1598) caused a more serious demographic fluctuation in East Asia than in Europe. Not only was the shrink of the population more severe than in Europe, but the speed of the increasing population is also very rapid after the war, due to the speedy economic recovery in East Asia.

Figure 2.3 shows the adult male population in the fifteenth century and Fig. 2.4 shows the total population in eighteenth century. The two figures invite comparison with the economic gravity between fifteenth century and eighteenth century, which show us where power plant is. Figure 2.3 indicates the population cluster in 1428. Seoul has the largest population, followed by Chongsŏng, nearby today's Vladivostok, Gilchu, and P'yŏngyang. This shows that most of the northern part of Korea, the birthplace of Jurchen tribe, has the largest population.

Table 2.1 shows the high rank of household, population, and taxable land in the fifteenth century. We can see most of them are in the northern part of Korea. The southwest Honam region is the ricebasket of Korea, but the population map clearly shows us that during the fifteenth century, it has a relatively lower population. The main reason for population being low in the ricebasket is due to annual invasions by Japanese pirate. The main phase of Japanese pirate activity was in the late fourteenth century to the early fifteenth century. Pirates from Japan focused their raids on the Korean Peninsula and spread across the Yellow Sea to China. According to Korean records, Japanese pirates were particularly rampant from around 1350. Their annual invasions of the ricebasket southern provinces of Chŏlla and Gyŏngsang explain the lack of an economically active population.

In physical geography, northern Korea is a type of biome where the food growth is hindered by low temperatures and drought of growing seasons. It is an "uplands" and "mountain tract" area. For example, Hamgyŏng Province (in present-day North Korea) had the lowest proportion of wet fields; the average proportion of wet fields and dry fields over its 22 counties and districts was 4.35 and 95.65%, respectively. The area in which the population was centered in the fifteenth century was considered a typical infertile region.

The gathering of the population in the northern part of Korea remains an open question. Is it a case of cultural fusion across the nomadic people or a separation from peninsula? Korea is geographically considered as a sub-peninsula of East Asia with China and Japan, which is bounded on the east, west, and south by the Pacific Ocean. It has always been an abiding aspect of Sinitic civilization. The fertile deltas of Han River, Kŭm River, and Yŏngsan River in the southern part of Korea have provided the agricultural foundation for all subsequent development, but in the north, the terrain was unsuitable for the settled agriculture. We can find the answer to this question in CFT.

For example, snow is very important icon for seasoned farmer's preparation of crop seed in CFT. The first chapter of CFT, "Preparing crops seed," states as follows:

> During the winter months, the seeds should be stored in an earthenware jar or wooden tub, (which is then) buried. It is imperative that (the contents) not freeze. In the last month of the (lunar) year, collect a sufficient

Table 2.1 10 high rank of household, population, and taxable land

Household			Population			Taxable land		
S	Chŏlla	Cheju 5207	N	Hamgyŏng	Chongsŏng 21,815	N	Pyŏngan	Pyŏngyang 48,160
N	Hamgyŏng	Hamhŭng 3538	N	Hamgyŏng	Kilchu 14,819	N	Hwanghae	Haechu 28,919
N	Pyŏngan	Anchu 2690	N	Pyŏngan	Pyŏngyang 14,440	N	Hamgyŏng	Hamhŭng 27,774
M	Kyŏnggi	Kanghwa 2445	S	Chungch'ŏng	Kongchu 10,049	N	Hwanghae	Pyŏngsan 20,727
N	Hamgyŏng	Yŏnghŭng 2191	N	Hamgyŏng	Kyŏngsŏng 9031	S	Chungch'ŏng	Ch'ungchu 19,893
S	Chungch'ŏng	Kongchu 2167	N	Hamgyŏng	Hamhŭng 8913	S	kyŏngsang	Kyŏngchu 19,733
N	Hwanghae	Pyŏngsan 2130	N	Pyŏngan	Anchu 8567	M	Kyŏnggi	Suwŏn 19,154
N	Hwanghae	Hwangchu 2034	N	Hamgyŏng	Yŏnghŭng 8524	S	Chŏlla	Chŏnchu 18,664
N	Hwanghae	Haechu 1926	S	Chŏlla	Taechŏng 8500	S	Chungch'ŏng	Kongchu 18,526

Source Geographical Appendix of the Veritable Records of King Sejong (GAVK, 1454)

Fig. 2.5 Arable land—ratio of dry fields and wet fields in the fifteenth century (Legend: **Dark** = Wet, **Bright** = Dry)

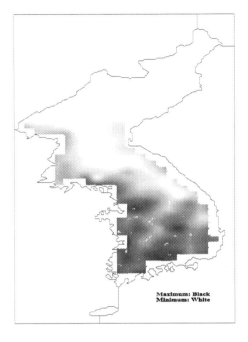

amount of melted snow, store it to the brim in a chŏmch'ŏn [known locally as nalgae].

The well-being of the seed depended primarily upon an adequate snowfall during the winter. The origin of the snow technique can be found in pastoral life. When a Song envoy visited Chathay in 1055, he thought that the Ch'i-tan oxen and horses sometimes reach maturity and sometimes do not, just as is the case in his country with the breeding of silkworms. He was surprised and asked for an explanation. The answer is highly related to snow. If there is snow, above which the grass still extends an inch or more, then the oxen and horses will come to successful maturity. If there is no snow, or if the snow covers the grass, they will not come to maturity. Like the maturity of the Ch'i-tan's oxen and horse, the first chapter of CFT considers the snowfall as the reason for prosperity or calamity (Figs. 2.5, 2.6).[6]

[6] Karl A. Wittfogel (1946, p. 126).

Fig. 2.6 Arable Land—ratio of dry fields and wet fields in the eighteenth century (Legend: **Dark**=Wet, **Bright**=Dry)

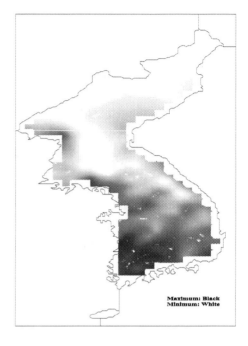

In the case of Chŏlla Province (in present-day South Korea) where there is the highest proportion of wet fields, the average proportion of wet fields and dry fields over its 56 counties and districts was 45.96% and 55.04, respectively. The proportion of dry fields is still quite high. In light of these geographical conditions, the core technique of the seasoned farmers is a hybrid between wet field farming and dry field farming. These techniques were highly respected in the fifteenth century. Thus, the intensive farming techniques based primarily on dry fields and the multi-cropping system demonstrate that it is the premier farming text of the fifteenth century.

Looking at Table 2.1, there is no evidence accounting for the shifting populations from the north by terrain unsuitable for the settled agriculture to the south taking advantage of the abundant availability of rice-growing land in the fifteenth century, but the story of snow tells us at least there was a semi-agricultural society in the northern part of Korea, and nomadic people easily changed their economic mentality from pastoralism to sedentary agriculture. Snow in CFT well encouraged them toward the sedentary life.

One of the conundrums in Korean economic history is the ruralization during the 1400–1900. What is important for any economic history of pre-modern Korea is that we have to investigate quantitative data on agricultural productivity, rural commercialization, and population growth and form a time series of prices, in short collect information on the four factors of importance in the development of a pre-modern economy. And we should combine this with forms of institutional change, such as private individual landownership, multi-geniture inheritance, highly organized rural goods and land markets, centralized government, Confucian ideology, etc.

The population rise in the begging of the fifteenth century put pressure on food prices, but after CFT printing out, rice prices relatively stabilized. Before the mid-1600s, property rights of land were not sufficiently protected, and infrastructure investment was too little to have a significant effect on the development of markets not tied to government. The imbalances between rice and cotton cloth prices in the sixteenth century probably indicate a systemic crisis: a devaluation of female labor with women increasingly relegated to childbearing that increased population with few preventive checks.

The Japanese invasion in the last decade of the sixteenth century decisively shattered society and devastated the population. The East Asian crisis resulted in great changes in state power which triggered the fall of the Ming dynasty in China (1644). After wars, the Korean government introduced the incentive of property rights in order to increase revenue. The rewards to be had in the land market caused an incentive to the farmers which brought about more efficiency. The new institution caused productivity to rise from the mid-seventeenth century to the end of the eighteenth century. Japan had suffered from the Korean government's banning policy before their invasion, but enjoyed the technological progress, political and institutional developments after the war that transformed war-torn Sengoku into the unified Tokugawa Bakufu system.

Since the Chosŏn government needed revenue for the recovery after 1600, it experimented with new policies to improve taxable agricultural production. Rising land values from the 1600s into the 1700s reflected expanded investment in land and a recovering population. From 1645, land rights were protected by law and massive investments began in irrigation and grain storage facilities. More valuable land and the protection of property rights supplied incentives to acquire land and increase food and non-food agricultural production for markets. One important result was the rise of a thriving land market that supplied the foundation for general economic diversification. Various products were developed, and female labor related to cotton cloth production became highly valued. Preventive checks on population (rather than positive checks like war, famine, and pestilence) allowed women to weave for the market, and the Korean system took on the characteristics of a Smithian model.

Private property rights received government protection, and the central government began heavy investments in irrigation, sea and river transport systems, and grain storage. Agricultural productivity expanded with more widespread transplantation of rice seedlings and with new harvesting regimes that boosted production.

An expansion of productivity up to about 1750 was followed by a stationary period (1750–1800), which was followed by a period of decline and diminishing returns (1800–1900). This project presents some initial issues of the agricultural foundation of Chosŏn dynasty. Takahashi summarizes Korea's historical agricultural regimes as multi-cropping systems. He had no doubt that Korea's complex and intensive systems filled an important role in the development of rural society in Chosŏn dynasty.

There was a resurgence of interest in crop rotation, intercropping, double-cropping, and mixed cropping during King Sejong's time (r. 1418–1450). The "continuous system" planted rice, barley, or beans this year and followed with the same next year. The "rotation system" alternated rice and barley over two years. The "combination system" added rotation to continuous cultivation and achieved three harvests every two years, far surpassing all other systems.

This difference in position, without enough rainfall seasons, made it possible for them to devise systems of agriculture whereby they grow two, three, and even four crops on the same piece of ground each year. In P'yŏngan Province, two crops of rice are grown; in the seaside region, there may be a crop of late-sowing rice; in the mountainous regions, there be a crop of early-sowing rice using terraced fields, in the following sequence: summer rice then winter barley (or vegetables) then summer rice (or beans) then winter barley (or vegetables), and so on, resulting in three grain crops over two spring-autumn planting-harvesting seasons.

For dry fields, the "combination" system produced summer millet (or beans) then winter wheat then summer beans (or green peas) then winter wheat, and so on, resulting in three crops (two possible grains and a legume) over two spring-autumn planting-harvesting seasons. What is notable is that after the Japanese invasions, fallow land was no longer permitted by law, and the general agricultural regime on the peninsula had achieved a sophisticated cropping system.

It is worth taking a moment here to comment on a possible connection between cultivation systems and population. The trend of Korean population shows that the period from 1650 to 1750 recorded the highest population growth rates in the world, just when the "combination" system was becoming widespread and government was embarking on a series of positive policies to improve agricultural production (protecting property rights and investing in irrigation, grain storage, and transport).

The sophisticated cropping system continued, but population stabilized over the subsequent stable period (1750–1800). Food and non-food prices also stabilized at the same time. Although there was more food and prices were stable, population reached a plateau, Jun's data (2007, 2008) show the decadal trend in grain prices. Grain prices were either high or unstable until the mid-1740s when they began to fall and are stabilized by the mid-1770s where they remained until the 1830s–1850s, when fluctuation began again, and a rising trend becomes apparent. Jun's data (2007) show a similar pattern for non-food goods: instability until the mid-1700s followed by a stable period until the mid-1800s.

The stability derived from government investment in infrastructure and grain storage and the coincident development of legal protection for property rights from 1645. These supports led to the development of markets. Markets acted as a damper on commodity price swings and a period of relatively stable prices was achieved from the mid-eighteenth century to the mid-nineteenth century.

The data argue that this period of relative stability can best be explained by a model based on Adam Smith's thought: expansion, stability, and decline. Expansion occurred in the period from 1430 to 1500. This was followed by stability from 1750 to 1800 or even 1850. Decline appeared with growing instability from the middle of the nineteenth century and is indicated by rising food prices, falling real wages, and falling real land values.

These trends meant a declining standard of living. In sum, the new "combination" agricultural regime produced wealth. Government investment in infrastructure and the protection of property rights bolstered and protected this wealth. The issue under consideration in this paper is how to explain the earlier trends from the fifteenth century up to the Japanese invasion of 1592. Using heterogeneous data from before

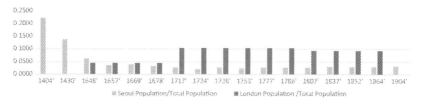

Fig. 2.7 Ruralization Korea vs Urbanization UK (1392–1910)

1600 to compare with homogenous data after 1600 is fraught with danger, but we have no choice until more accurate data are available for the period before the Japanese invasion (Fig. 2.7).

The land prices and rice prices of pre-modern Korea are well documented compared to other price information. Korea achieved substantial political stability after 1650 and up until 1850. There was little internal or external war, which can be proven by the abundance of profitable land sale documents and account books reflecting the development of rural markets, but it is impossible to get an estimate of real farm day wages using well-documented data.

Figure 2.8 shows the relationship between Real Value of Land (RVL) and the size of population. It uses RVL as the available evidence on the productivity of pre-modern Korea. As Fig. 2.8 shows, there is a strong positive correlation between RVL and the growing rate of population. Of course, over time, the speed with which population grows is what determines how many people there are. But the period makes a difference; during the 1600s–1650s, the population is decreasing, but RVL is increasing, then from the 1650s–1700s both the population and RVL rapidly increase, and then in the 1700s–1750s, there is a relatively stagnated RVL with growing population. This means RVL series versus population numbers reject the Malthusian model.

Figure 2.8 sparks a rethinking of the Malthusian model and Adam Smithian model for pre-modern Korea, but we cannot find any trade-off between higher population and a lower RLV. The seventeenth and eighteenth centuries were eras in which efficiency advances appear very clear in comparison with the mid-nineteenth century, which was continuously affected by famine, disease, riots, and climatic shock, and the early sixteenth century which found Korea in wars. The economy in the nineteenth century underlies the positive checks of the Malthusian

2 CHOSON'S SETTLED POPULATION BY KING'S REIGN (1392–1910) 37

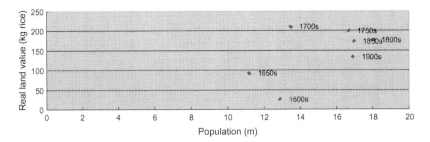

Fig. 2.8 Real land value vs population (1550–1910) (*Source* Jun Seong Ho, "Wages, Rents, and Interest Rates in Southern Korea, 1700 to 1900," *Research in Economic History*, Vol. 24. Presented in WEHC Helsinki 2006, Session 21, 52)

model, but the expansion of the Korean economy in the seventeenth and eighteenth centuries was largely the product of increased birthrates or falling death rates combined with technological advance and commercial advance, as suggested by Adam Smith. Institutional change in particular seems to have made a large impact on incentives.

REFERENCES

Karl A. Wittgogel. *History of Chinese Society Liao (907–1125)*. American Philosophical Society. 1946.

Peter Lee. *A History of Korean Literature*. Cambridge, UK: Cambridge University Press, 2003.

CHAPTER 3

What Climatic Change During the First Global Age Tells Us

Climate scientists actively work to understand our earth's past and future climate by using observations like growth rings of old trees, the rocks made by volcanic activities, and earth surface temperatures to study a climate history. Their research gives us a glimpse into the historical changes of global wave spanned eleventh through twenty-first centuries.

The fifteenth century is not only the mid-point of the past millennium, but also recorded the lowest summer temperatures. The long-lasting period that is explored in this book is defined by the initial onset of the Black Death in Europe.[1] This coincides with the darkest times in the Middle Ages of Europe from the fourteenth through the fifteenth centuries, was stricken by the wars, great famine, and the spread of contagious diseases.

Turning to the neighboring Japan, the fifteenth century was right in the middle of *Muromachi* era (1336–1573), also known for having the highest frequency of famine in the 1000 years from the tenth to the twentieth centuries. Like Europe, Japan came to create a "Malthusian virtue" for the survival of the fittest through constant wars. During the period, Japanese people developed swordsmanship that killed humans in civil wars, much like the hundred years' war running from 1337 to 1453 in Europe. Japan entered a dark era with a decline in literary work to express human minds and scientific writings.

---

[1] Kevin H. O'Rourke (2007, p. 87).

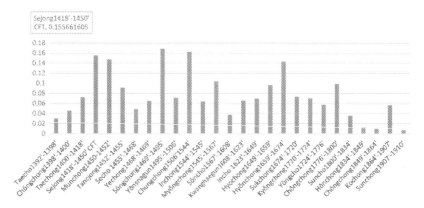

Fig. 3.1 Total frequency of national disasters divided by King's reigning days

At that time Japan suffered from the Kansho famine (1459–1460), which led to the Onin War (1467–1477), the destruction of the capital city Kyoto, which ultimately led Japan to become an aggregate of warring states. Overall, multi-decadal temperature variability from the twelfth to fifteenth centuries appears to have resulted in many serious societal disturbances.[2]

During the beginning of the fifteenth century, East Asia also suffered from extreme starvation due to droughts. For example, in 1419, the terrible drought s caused the death-by-starvation of as many as 140,000 people in Ch'ungch'ŏng Province and 12,223 in Hamgil Province of Korea.

Figure 3.1 shows the number of recorded natural disasters such as droughts, floods, winds, damage caused by harmful insects, and famines that occurred during Chosŏn Korea. It reported a total of 1794 cases during King Sejong's reign (1418–1450) and 1542 cases during King Seongjong's reign (1462–1495). As indicated in Fig. 3.1, the period just after the enthronement of King Sejong marked the highest recorded natural disaster and famine reports when divided by total number of days in power. The abnormal summer temperatures from 1417 to 1426 resulted in poor harvests across the nation, causing famines. According to the research, pests affected the countries in Central Asia and Europe starting from the mid-to-late fourteenth century, peaked in the fifteenth century,

[2] William Wayne Farris (2009, p. 3).

and started to decline by the seventeenth century. The disease was the force behind a sharp population decline in the regions.

However, why did the great famine in the fifteenth century not result in "Malthusian virtue" in Chosŏn Korea? This book looks to find an answer to this question, as well as explains an intensive system for the expansion of tillage and food production. Chosŏn Korea created remarkable land-use systems which are rich in significant diversity evolving from the co-adaptation of a community with its environment.

The development of food production can be recognized in a context of Confucian knowledge networks in the fifteenth century. The fifteenth century during the reign of King Sejong was representative of the Confucian renaissance as it was a time period within Korean history with unprecedented advances in multiple areas. Confucianism indicated that through an elaborate fiscal system, an enhancement of fiduciary responsibility of the central government can be achieved simultaneously with an increase in well-being of the peasants.

To meet the challenge of producing more food from the mountainous resources, traditional seasoned farmers' experiences were required. To achieve a high level of production, there is need to know the ideal water amount, temperature, and photoperiod regulation of rice, which is key for a high potential yield. The Chosŏn government led the establishment of an agricultural knowledge system and published many books in cooperation with the seasoned farmer. Among many publications published in the fifteenth century, two were related to agriculture in particular.

The compilation of one of these two publications, CFT, was ordered by King Sejong in the first half of the fifteenth century. It contains a great amount of valuable farming knowledge and was amazed at great effort with the objective of spreading this knowledge to establish an agricultural method more in accordance with the geography and climate of the Korean Peninsula.

Moreover, its value is not only historical but also linguistic and social, as it reflects the concerns for subsistence, the daily lives of people at that time, their customs and dietary habits, and their work ethic. Similarly, the mere existence of this compilation reveals the will of the king to push the peninsula's inhabitants to strive to achieve "the great agricultural states under Heaven" from the methods employed by other countries, such as China, Vietnam, and India. However, these countries had different geographic features and climatic conditions that could not be superposed to a territory with its own needs and customs.

Although imported methods served as reference and contributed to enrich the customs of agriculture in Korea for years, they could not help entirely overcome country's own limitations. Therefore, there was a need to establish new and improved ways to respond to the challenges that its territory encountered, patiently coming up with inventive solutions that seasoned farmers adopted into their daily labor and passed down from generation to generation.

The court of the Chosŏn dynasty started to disseminate farming books and established the monetary system for small peasants. King Taejong (r. 1400–1418) conducted a project to spread the farming books imported from China. Moving beyond importing and mimicking the Chinese farming techniques, King Sejong (r. 1418–1450) explored local farming techniques adequate to local soil under climate conditions and farming cycles different from their Chinese counterparts. He ordered a compilation of farming information into a book and printed these books to provide for all provinces across the country. The printing of books with the purpose of spreading useful information was rare in other parts of the world in the fifteenth century. This can be regarded as "Smithian virtue" of the fifteenth-century Chosŏn society renaissance.

Along with ordering the compilation of variable experiences of the seasoned farmers, King Sejong also ordered making a census categorizing all land as an arable or wasteland and dividing them into proportions suitable for wet field and dry field farming by counties and districts and created statistical data of this information. The census may be the world's first comprehensive census. The statistics of numbers of households per county and district and the area of arable land have been worked into the irrigated lowland (southern Korea seaside land), non-stressed upland (southern Korea inland), moderately stressed upland (middle part of Korea), severely water-stressed upland (northern part Korea) (see Appendix C: GAVK).

References

Kevin H. O'Rourke. *Power and Plenty Trade, War, and the World Economy in the Second Millennium.* Princeton and Oxford: Princeton University Press, 2007.

William Wayne Farris. *Daily Life and Demographics in Ancient Japan Michigan.* Monograph Series in Japanese Studies (No. 63), 2009.

CHAPTER 4

Emerging Seed Science in CFT

The soil conditions of Kzyl-Orda Oblast in fact proved to guarantee a high production of rice which all the rice seeds are germinated between May 1 and 25. Taking this fact into account it is important to combine two different methods; planting seeds in the early spring deeply and watering directly after having sown them. Normally they are sown at a depth 1.5-2cm. The essence of sowing them in the early spring lies in the carrying out of sowing when the temperature of the ground at a depth 10 cm reaches 8°C. Rice seeds sown at a depth of 4-6 cm will burgeon from the moisture stored in ground.[1]

The emergence of grain seeds in international trade and diplomacy in the fifteenth century not only indicated the climatic change, but also served as contributing factor to the birth of the seed science. The Ming dispatched diplomatic envoys to Chosŏn in the fifteenth century, mainly to ask about the seeds of rice especially early-sowing rice. This illustrates that the seeds were subject to special management by the government and that their management was considered as a diplomatic affair. Domestically, seeds were subject to special management in that the state should prepare seeds beforehand in case of natural disasters.

In 1424, King Sejong instructed the Ministry of Taxation to give special supplies to all households in eight provinces, Kyŏnggi, Ch'ungch'ŏng, Chŏlla, Kyŏngsang, Hwanghae, P'yŏngan, Kangwŏn,

---

[1] Soviet daily newspaper in Korean, the *Lenin Kichi* (1938–1990). April 28, 1983, p. 2.

© The Author(s) 2019
S. H. Jun, *Agriculture and Korean Economic History*,
https://doi.org/10.1007/978-981-32-9319-9_4

and Hamgil, all of which were requesting seeds and staples, and to report the quantities provided. He was worried that the seeds to be used for farming would be eaten since the provinces had suffered from famine the previous year and reserves were low. If this happened, the quantity of planting seeds would be insufficient at planting time that year, making farming impossible. If there were insufficient seeds for planting, then there would be a series of hunger years, and the famine would recur. Therefore, in order to prevent such a vicious circle, seeds were provided in accordance with the proper seasons. In other words, providing seeds in accordance with the timing of the planting season was a special measure taken at the state level to prevent the greatest crisis.[2]

A royal edict was sent to the eight provinces that read, "I have sent an office warrant saying, 'timely reports should be made if there are shortages of seeds and food among people.' I have heard that there are some who cannot farm because of insufficient seeds. Estimate the quantities of seeds needed by such households and give them seeds to encourage sowing and report the quantities of seeds that are distributed."

As we can see, the nation's top leader made the "securing of seeds" a top priority of national policy in the fifteenth century, when natural disasters occurred one after another. The importance of seeds was also keenly recognized at the state level when the Ming dynasty demanded seeds. We can easily assume that the reason why seed preparation is discussed in Chapter 1 of the CFT, which stems from the fact that the Ming had on several occasions demanded seeds during the fifteenth century.

We know the Ming's demands arrived in 1423, 1430, and 1431. In 1423 specifically, the Ming's envoy demanded, in their trade items, about 900 liters (local unit *sŏm*) of early-ripening varieties and 450 liters of late-ripening varieties. In this year, Sejong delivered a royal edict to order the governor of P'yŏngan to carry the rice varieties requested by the Ming envoy to Ŭiju in advance and wait with them.[3] In 1430, Yun Pong is naturalized eunuch official of the Ming Dynasty who was born in Chosŏn Hwanghae Province was sent to Chosŏn as an envoy 10 times, especially during the reign of King Sejong. He demanded 180 liters of early-sowing rice.[4]

---

[2] Annals of King Sejong, 06/05/06 1424.
[3] Annals of King Sejong, 05/09/02 1423.
[4] Annals of King Sejong, 13/09/08 1431.

This is one of the most famous cases where the Chinese imperial court demanded and obtained early-sowing varieties from other countries. The origin of these varieties is known to be the Vietnamese mountain area where the rice terraces had been developed. They were imported from this region with special care by the Song dynasty in the eleventh century and successfully produced in China. Ping-Ti Ho describes the technology as "the core of the 'agricultural revolution' in early-modern East Asia" and as a core technology in the history of China's scientific and technological development that is more important than water control and irrigation projects for agricultural land.[5]

Some of the most important information contained in CFT is the finding of the optimum time for planting, because most crops such as rice, barley, bean, and wheat that are seeded too late or too early have lower or higher yield potential no matter how they are cultivated after planting. For example, early-sowing varieties are planted as soon as possible for high yield. Therefore, the entire information contained in CFT refers to deciding on determining a planting date for all crops. The central technologies in CFT that resulted in the Industrious Revolution taking place in fifteenth-century Korea were the development of early-sowing rice varieties, legume double-cropping, and dry farming for rice to weather drought.

The origin of early-sowing rice varieties as known today is from the terraced rice paddies of Vietnam's mountainous areas, which were especially sought out by the Song emperor in the eleventh century and imported into China, where it became a productive crop variety. This technology became the core of the Agricultural Revolution in early-modern East Asia and is described as being of greater importance than irrigation technologies for farmland in the history of China's development of scientific technologies.

Descriptions of these varieties in agricultural treatises disappeared during the thirteenth to fourteenth centuries with the rule of the Mongol Empire over China and appeared again in fifteenth-century Korea in CFT as the core variety in the new technological developments of that time period. As these early-sowing rice varieties were especially demanded by Ming China and traded for Chinese silk, the intent behind compiling CFT was not to develop Korea's food production, but for

---

[5] Ping-Ti Ho (1956, p. 201).

international diplomacy and commerce, as this English translation project of the text demonstrates.

In addition, attention is also paid to the major role played by Korea's empirical science in the development of technologies to fulfill China's demand for rice as well as the names of these varieties and farming tools listed in CFT that are totally different than those listed in Chinese farming texts. CFT highlights how experienced Korean farmers developed the technologies to plant and grow these new varieties. Thus, this project emphasizes how important it was to King Sejong that he institutionalized a method of communication in order to develop the farmers' empirical knowledge as a new scientific technology led by the state.

In other words, the empirical knowledge of Korea's "seasoned farmers" was of utmost importance to develop the technologies to plant and grow early-sowing rice varieties, which King Sejong realized could only be done through a phonetic alphabet system rather than in Chinese characters, resulting in the invention of *hangŭl*.

This book presents the historical link between the compilation of *CFT* and the invention of *hangŭl* through supporting historical records, highlighting the fact that Korea's seasoned farmers possessed the creative technologies earnestly sought by the state in the fifteenth century. The development technologies for early-sowing rice varieties in fifteenth-century Korea are explained as the origin of extremely rapid population growth and the development of labor-intensive industries which continued until the eighteenth century in East Asia's Industrious Revolution.[6]

Furthermore, Western scholars of East Asia also define this as the "high-equilibrium trap."[7] The Industrious Revolution theory, following Jan de Vries and Gary Becker's "A Theory of the Allocation of Time," argues that the advent of the most basic commodities to fulfill the utility functions of household budgets in Europe created production efficiency and consumption efficiency and increased the markets for domestic demand and exports.

The importation and imitation of East Asian luxury goods in seventeenth-century and eighteenth-century Europe brought about new revolutions in pigmentation and design technologies, achieving explosive growth in export-led, import-substitution development and leading

---

[6] Kaoru Sugihara (2003, Chapter 3, pp. 78–123).
[7] Mark Elvin (1973, p. 298).

to the unprecedented increase in production that was the Industrial Revolution. The Industrious Revolution in fifteenth-century Korea approximates the Imitation-Innovation-Invention path that arose in seventeenth-century to eighteenth-century England.

The Imitation-Innovation-Invention path, a model advocated by Maxine Berg, explains the Industrious Revolution, which was the historical origin of the Industrial Revolution, as the process of imitation to innovation that first took place in seventeen-century to eighteenth-century agricultural England and expanded all over Europe. The difference between the Industrious Revolution in fifteenth-century Korea and seventeenth-century Europe was the latter resulted in the Industrial Revolution while the former resulted in the Agriculture Revolution.[8]

However, both share the commonality of households as the units of production based on agricultural societies. Moreover, both overcame the inefficient division of time of the off-season and farming season in traditional agricultural societies and saw revolutions in efficiency based on the exact measurement of time. Lastly, they also had export-led growth from import substitution.

Before the Industrial Revolution began in the nineteenth century, Europe was already infatuated with imitating commodities purchased from East Asia and attempted to substitute imports mainly by having their craftsmen newly designed and dye imported commodities. At the center of this import substitution was continual revolution and invention, systemizing science into the manufacturing process and finally leading to exporting their own commodities and their dominance in the world market for scientific technologies until the twentieth century.

This was the same as King Sejong exporting newly invented knowledge to Ming China based on the efforts of his predecessor, King Taejong, who imported as much knowledge as possible from Ming China in the fifteenth century and imitated that knowledge in a sort of import substitution. This story sheds light on the paths of Imitation-Innovation-Invention and the Industrious Revolution by focusing on the compilation of CFT in King Sejong's reign in the fifteenth century.

Farming household budgets and farmland in fifteenth-century Korea were spaces for living, reproduction, and intergenerational interaction and the units in which family members combined their allocation of

---

[8] Maxine Berg (2002, pp. 1–30).

resources efficiently. Thus, they can be seen as the driving force of the Industrious Revolution.[9]

In the same way, the materials introduced in CFT were necessities for the management of daily life in fifteenth-century Korea. These items could be sufficiently produced and consumed by villages since the fifteenth century, but they were also purchased at the market. Daily necessities such as the main staple of rice as well as clothing and other products were used in transactions in the marketplace, and the expansion of the market for rice exports, a phenomenon resembling the Industrious Revolution that took place in seventeenth-century to eighteenth-century Europe, can be seen around the time of the compilation of CFT in the fifteenth century.

The story explains the establishment of new agricultural state institutions in the fifteenth century and its link to the compilation of CFT's planting and growing technologies of early-sowing rice varieties leading to the rise of new agricultural systems, and the transition from importing to exporting. Taking the case of early-sowing rice varieties that were the core of CFT into consideration, we can see that the Industrious Revolution took place in fifteenth-century Korea through the development of growing and planting technologies that aimed to maximize harvests by reallocating productive labor time to avoid droughts, floods, and strong winds and aim for stable harvests.[10]

The story should follow the logic of Imitation-Innovation-Invention. First, the period from King Taejong's reign before the compilation of *CFT* in the fifteenth century will be defined as the stage of importing and imitating Chinese farming texts. Chinese characters play the primary role in this stage of importing and imitation. The stage of imitating Chinese knowledge in King Taejong's time encountered new conditions with King Sejong's reign. King Sejong knew that Chinese farming knowledge was unsuitable for the topographical conditions of Korea and opened a new innovative stage of adapting Chinese techniques to Korean conditions by synthesizing the agricultural techniques long utilized by farmers, the product of which was CFT.

However, Sejong realized a new language not based on Chinese characters was needed for this innovative product to reach Korean farmers.

---

[9] Jan de Vries (2008, pp. 85–132).

[10] The non-early-sowing grain varieties in CFT are hemp, barley, sesame, and buckwheat.

Thus, the next stage of invention was achieved with the creation of a new national language, *hangŭl*. This is proven by the publication of MKD, which is the book of seed science marked in *hangŭl* and its expansion in the eighteenth and nineteenth centuries.

The need for a new language system in the form of *hangŭl* transition from the imitation stage to the invention stage can be seen throughout CFT. For example, the categories on early-ripening rice varieties, sesame seeds, buckwheat, and millet are written in the vernacular language. These categories were newly expanded in the late nineteenth century in *Oju yŏnmun jangjŏn san'go*[11] and *Imwŏn gyŏngjeji*,[12] and *Yŏn gyŏngjae jŏnjip*,[13] as well as other important agricultural science texts until the eighteenth and nineteenth centuries, and the transcription of the *Kŭmyang japnok* MKD into *hangŭl* until the eighteenth century shows us the link between *hangŭl* and seed science.

The Chinese character for morning is *cho*,[14] while the character for early is *cho*.[15] The early-sowing rice in *CFT* was written as *choto*[16] before the creation of *hangŭl*, but in *MKD* was recorded according to the native Korean language as *olbyŏ*, *olibyŏ*, and *ilŭnbyŏ* after the invention of *hangŭl*. In Korean, *ol*, *oli*, *ilun*, *achim*, and *iltchick* referred to the concept of "early," "soon," "morning," the concept, which can be seen in the name of Asadal in *Memorabilia of the Three Kingdoms* or the Japanese *Asahi* newspaper and *Waseda* University shows that it is still widely used in both Korea and Japan.[17]

Ŏromgŏtki is explained as a variety that can be sown as soon as the ice has melted, which can be easily known by anyone who reads it in *hangŭl*. In addition, *kuhwangteori* means that this was an early-sowing rice harvested during the period of low grain production known as "barley hill," i.e., the off-season after the barley harvest and before the rice harvest. In this way, *hangŭl* labels were conducive to easily understanding knowledge for varieties.

---

[11] 五洲衍文長箋散稿.
[12] 林園經濟志.
[13] 研經齋全集.
[14] 朝.
[15] 早.
[16] 早稻.
[17] *Samguksagi Vol. 1* (三國史記 卷1 脫解尼師今).

CFT aimed for a seed science conciseness that could convey the most concise knowledge on farming that could not be expressed by Chinese characters was aided by hangŭl. The power of this concise delivery of knowledge is shown in eighteenth-century through nineteenth-century publications that labeled hundreds of rice varieties in hangŭl. As seen in MKD, the number of rice variety labels in hangŭl from the early Chosŏn to rapidly increases into the late Chosŏn period.

For example, the early-sowing rice variety *Kyemyŏngdo* is labeled in hangŭl as *talguri* in *Yŏn gyŏngjae jŏnjip*, as *talgorye* in *Chŭngbo sallim gyŏngje*, as *talgyuri* in *Oju yŏnmun jangjŏn san'go*, and as *talguri* in *Imwŏn gyŏngjeji*. The early-sowing varieties are all part of the "*ol*," "*ori*," group phonetically meaning is early- and the late-sowing varieties of rice are all written as "*nori*," "*nŭri*," phonetically meaning is evening or late. Examining the time spans of phonetic labels of grain in Chinese and hangŭl shows us that the 1402 translation of CEA[18] during King Taejong's reign (1400–1418) and the compilation of CFT during King Sejong's reign are about 27 years, the time span between CFT and the invention of hangŭl in 1443 was about 14 years, and the time span between hangŭl and MKD was about 50 years, which continued to extend for over three to four hundred years into the eighteenth and nineteenth centuries.

From this, it is clear that the compilation of CFT was the starting point for the invention of hangŭl, the latter of which was central to the longevity of these grain labels. According to the development path of Imitation-Innovation-Invention, importing CEA was part of the imitation stage, and King Sejong's realization of the difference in topography between Korea and China brought about the innovation of CFT (1419–1429), while the publishing of *Calculation of the Motions of the Seven Celestial Determinants* (Ch'ilchŏngsan[19] 1433), the expansion of Hamgil Province and metal typography (1434), the invention and installation of rain measures (1442), the invention and promulgation of hangŭl (1443 and 1446, respectively), and the labeling of grains in hangŭl in MKD (1492), were part of the innovation stage.

What were the economic factors distinguishing early-sowing rice varieties into "*ol*" and "*ori*," and late-sowing varieties as "*nori*" and "*nŭri*"?

---

[18]This is the first text on farming compiled under the auspices of the state, begun in 1273 and published in 1286.

[19]七政算.

If one traces back the names of grains labeled in eighteenth-century and nineteenth-century farming texts as shown in CFT, although CFT has labeled late-sowing varieties in Chinese characters, it also records the native Korean pronunciations of *ori* and *nŭri* and the extremely important descriptions accompanying them, which can be regarded as King Sejong intuiting the crucial impasse of communicating these technical systems. The core techniques conveyed by farmers had to coincide with the appropriate times for germination, planting, sowing, and other processes in a race against time.

Thus, King Sejong insightfully saw that techniques to increase food production were based on timing these techniques, as evidenced in the foreword of CFT which notes that "crop yields depend entirely on timing." Following this, the "ori" branch of grains is recorded as doubling food productivity. Therefore, the core technique that led to increased food production and solved the food shortages, pronounced as *ori* and conveyed to King Sejong by the famers was also divided into the best, acceptable, and worst periods for planting them by King Sejong. In this way, the central emphasis on timing placed by Sejong can be said to be the units of "efficiency" in which economic activities were maximized by the allocation of resources in the farm household budgets and productive farmlands that were the central spaces that linked living spaces, reproduction, and family generations and formed the heart of the Industrious Revolution.

King Sejong also highly emphasized the point that "crop yields depend entirely on timing," as the droughts afflicted every province in the early years of his reign since his ascension to the throne in 1419, which was five years after the importing of CEA to Korea.

This led to a rapid increase in the price of rice on the market due to natural disasters which persisted until the publication of CFT in 1429.[20] Hence, Sejong acutely felt the limits of the use of farming texts that did not have in mind Korea's topography, and adopted the farming techniques of Korean farmers, which is reflected in the main body of CFT which records the experiences of these farmers' methods of overcoming drought and distinguishing the times to sow and harvest early- and late-sowing grains. This can be viewed as the primary motivation behind

---

[20] Jun and Lewis (2008, pp. 244–282).

the move toward innovation rather than importing that was practiced in King Taejong's reign.

Another motivation was the increase in production from sowing as early as possible which led to increased harvests. King Sejong paid attention to the fact that when sowing early, the grain rather than the stalks absorbed the nutrients. Although CFT especially focuses on planting and growing techniques for early-sowing rice, King Sejong sought to spread the knowledge that "the earlier the sowing, the greater the harvest," based on the experiences of farmers all over the country.

The last motivation was to avoid chronic natural disasters such as the drought during the sowing period and floods and winds in the harvest period through the safest method of developing early-sowing grains. This resulted in doubled production and King Sejong found a guaranteed method to avoid the droughts in the fourth and fifth months (of the lunar calendar), heavy rains in the seventh and eighth months, and typhoons in the eighth and ninth months.

The method of developing new knowledge in the foreword of CFT was the collating and standardizing by the state of the experiences of farmers from all over the country. This continued after CFT in its subsequent revised and updated editions as well as in MKD, the former of which focused on how to sow early, late, and drought-resistant grain varieties while the latter was a development manual on how to grow certain types of grain.

REFERENCES

Jan De Vries. The Industrial Revolution and the Industrious Revolution. *The Journal of Economic History*, Vol. 54, No. 2, pp. 249–270, June 1994.

Jan De Vries. *The Industrious Revolution: Consumer Behavior and the Household Economy, 1650 to the Present*. New York: Cambridge University Press, 2008.

Jun Seong Ho and James B. Lewis. Korean Expansion and Decline from the Seventeenth to the Nineteenth Century: A View Suggested by Adam Smith. *Journal of Economic History*, Vol. 68, No. 1, pp. 244–282, 2008.

Kaoru Sugihara. The East Asian Path of Economic Development: A Long-Term Perspective. In *The Resurgence of East Asia 500, 150 and 50 Year Perspectives*, Chapter 3, pp. 78–123. Edited by Giovanni Arrighi, Takeshi Hamashita, and Mark Selden. London: RoutledgeCurzon, 2003.

Mark Elvin. *Pattern of the Chinese Past: A Social and Economic Interpretation*. Stanford: Stanford University Press, 1973.

Maxine Berg. From Imitation to Invention: Creating Commodities in Eighteenth-Century Britain. *The Economic History Review*, New Series, Vol. 55, No. 1, pp. 1–30, 2002.

Ping-Ti Ho. Early-Ripening Rice in Chinese History. *The Economic History Review*, Vol. 9, No. 2, pp. 200–218, 1956.

CHAPTER 5

Drought: Enduring and Leguminous Plants Science

F. H. King's *Farmers of Forty Centuries* was a famous book of study and travel in rural regions of China, Korea, and Japan in 1911. King sought the everlasting way to maintain fertility to produce sufficiently for the maintenance of such dense populations, but it is a misfortune that King did not touch enough on the case of Korea and its mountainous land.

> It was not until 1888 and then after a prolonged war of more than thirty years, generaled by the best scientists of all Europe, that it was finally conceded as demonstrated that leguminous plants acting as hosts for lower organisms living on their roots are largely responsible for the maintenance of soil nitrogen, drawing it directly from the air to which it is returned through the processes of decay. But centuries of practice had taught the Far East farmers that the culture and use of these crops are essential to enduring fertility, and so in each of the three countries the growing of legumes in rotation with other crops very extensively for the express purpose of fertilizing the soil is one of their old, fixed practices. (F. H. King 1911, Introduction)

F. H. King in the early twentieth century spent time nearby rice fields during his journeys, strongly noted that the Korean characteristics, usually under better and more intensified culture, were slightly more advanced than Japan. The plowing in Japan was done mostly with horses instead of the oxen used in Korea. He also sought the microorganisms in biofertilizers mutually returning the soil's natural nutrient cycle.

King thought the Japanese agriculture was derived from Korea. At that time, various Japanese agricultural economists pondered the Korean case, because the question was sensitive for the Japanese Empire, which annexed Korea as a planned agricultural colony between 1910 and 1945.

Takahashi Noboru in 1918 graduate of Tokyo University's Faculty of Agriculture argued in the mid- to late-1930s that Japan should appreciate Korean complexities for the regenerative agriculture created in the traditional Korean rural area and the achievements of Korean agricultural experience. He proposed abandoning the imposition of Japanese-derived monoculturing models and, in essence, argued for abandoning the colonial policy forced into rice monoculture.

When his extensive field study of Korean agriculture was reprinted in 1998, one of the editors, Kuiinuma Jirō, wrote in his introduction that his 45 years of study had taught him that the modernization of agriculture can only succeed if it is based on locally developed tradition. These scholars concluded that the Japanese Empire's focus on expanding wet rice mono-cultivation was inappropriate to the circumstances and that Korean traditional agriculture had achieved high productivity through a judicious mix of dry and wet fields with beans and barley playing a more versatile and stable role than rice. He admired King Sejong's national project concerning the multiple cropping systems in the fifteenth century as described in CFT.

But centuries of practice had taught the Far East farmers that the culture and use of these crops are essential to enduring fertility, and so in each of the three countries, the growing of legumes in rotation with other crops very extensively for the express purpose of fertilizing the soil is one of their old, fixed practices.

Seasoned farmers from the northern part of Korea in fifteenth century recognized the hydrological environment was a combination of an irrigated yield system and adaptation to aerobic soils. Most of North Korea is upland rice-growing areas, and soils are infertile. In CFT, seasoned farmers point out that urine, a good source of nitrogen, has been successfully used to fertilize crops. This book evaluates the use of urine and ash as fertilizers for crops' cultivation and the seed treatment directly covered with a mixture of urine and ash.

A person excretes about 300 grams of feces and 1 liter of urine in a day. Traditional Korean toilets, especially northern part of Korean toilets, which take into consideration hygiene knowledge and ecological sanitation, are found to be suitable in the community where there is a use for urine and feces with ash. Unlike other East Asian countries, this is possible in Korea because of the efficient heating and cooking system based on *ondol*, and underfloor heating system which uses the fire of the kitchen to heat the house and produces ash on a daily basis in the process. Convention of the *ondol* has been found at archeological sites in upland present-day North Korea Hamgyŏng Province and Alaska's Aleutian Islands, which is an archeological dig at Unalaska revealing remains of a heated floor system with radiocarbon dating showing remains to be around 3000 years old.[1]

Do the farming techniques in CFT focus on dry field farming or wet field farming? First, the statistics in GAVK compiled in 1454 during the reign of King Danjong need to be recreated in order to answer this question. Along with ordering the compilation of CFT, King Sejong classified the arable land of the country into proportions suitable for wet field and dry field farming by counties and districts and created statistical data of this information. The data of numbers of households per county and district and the area of arable land from GAVK have been reworked into the contemporary statistics presented here. In the case of Hamgyŏng Province, which had the lowest proportion of wet fields, the average proportions of wet fields and dry fields over its 22 counties and districts were 4.35 and 95.65%, respectively.

In the case of Chŏlla Province, which had the highest proportion of wet fields, the average proportions of wet fields and dry fields over its 56 counties and districts were 45.96% and 55.04%, respectively. However, the proportion of dry fields is still quite high. In light of these geographical conditions, the core techniques in CFT are a combination of wet field rice farming and dry field farming techniques. As seen from the statistical data based on GAVK, the distribution of dry fields composes the majority of Chosŏn's land area, and thus, the intensive farming techniques based primarily on dry fields and multi-cropping system in CFT demonstrate that it is the premier farming text of the fifteenth century.

The combination of wet field rice farming and dry field farming techniques, which are not seen in the farming techniques of northern or southern China, is native to Chosŏn, and this is demonstrated by the vernacular names of techniques presented by CFT in 1429. For example, the sowing methods in CFT can be broadly classified into three categories. The first method uses water and is the wet farming method of growing rice paddies, the second is the dry farming method of growing

---

[1] Bean et al. (2010, p. 41).

dry rice paddies during droughts, and the last method is the modern seedling method. Each is introduced with its vernacular name, *musalmi*, *malŭnsalmi*, and *myojong*, respectively.

Although the wet farming method is introduced by its vernacular name of *musalmi* in CFT, it is introduced as the "Koryŏ's wet farming method" in Kim Sŏkju's 1683 anthology of works. After returning from Qing as an envoy in 1683, Kim wrote a record of his travels, which contains an account describing the only farm in the vast plains of Liaodong that farmed rice despite the dryland. This farm was run by a Korean and everyone called the technique he used to farm the rice the "Koryŏ wet farming method" and said that it originated from Koryŏ. In addition, it is quite interesting that Kim mentions the "fire weeding method"[2] used in wet farming in contrast to the "water weeding method"[3] using water.

In order to implement the *musalmi* (wet farming) method, CFT emphasizes the importance of selecting fertile paddies with a water source. Once this is done, then farming begins immediately with the start of the Lunar New Year, once the ice melts, which is an extremely laborious method as the winter farming off-season cannot be overlooked.

Whenever weeds are removed with the *musalmi* method, the water is drained and supplied again, and when the seeds are young, relatively little water is used and the weeds are picked by hand instead of with a hoe. Therefore, this method is convenient for terrace farming in mountainous areas where water from valleys can be continuously supplied and drained; it thus came to be called the "Chosŏn wet farming method" in the mountainous regions of China for growing early-sowing rice.[4]

---

[2] The "fire weeding method" (*hwanu*, 火耨) is missing from the 1581 edition of CFT but appears in the 1655 edition, and consists of removing weeds by first draining the paddies when the rice plants have sprouted about six leaves and then evenly spreading dry grass around the plants, after which fire is applied and then the paddies are supplied with water again. Although the "wet farming method" introduced in CFT uses only water and human hands to remove weeds one by one, the "fire weeding method" uses both water and fire to conveniently remove weeds over large farming areas. Ja Ock Guh and Yong In Kuk (2011, pp. 1–7).

[3] Sikam sŏnsaeng yuko (息庵先生遺稿), Vol 6, p. 27.

[4] A similar method to the *musalmi* method in *Theory* is introduced by eighteenth-century Kongju classics licentiate Yu Jinmuk as *hŏsalmi* (虛沙彌). This method plows the fields again to reduce the work of weeding after the seedlings are removed when it comes time to transplant them after they have grown in the fields, thus allowing them to be harvested as if they were directly sown. Yu mentions that this method does not appear in *Compilations for Farmers*. See *The Record of Daily Reflections* (Ilsŏngnok), Month 12, Day 16, 1798.

The representative dry field farming technique in CFT is known as *kŭlugali* (根耕) in the vernacular which is a kind of root nodules of legume crops and makes them available to the plants compound cropping which is the growing of two or more crop species where part or all of their crop cycle overlaps spatially, where more of the component species is taken to harvest. For example, rhizobia are soil bacteria which are able to colonize the legume roots and fix the atmospheric nitrogen symbiotically; the method of using barley and wheat roots in the process of sowing soybeans and red beans is the most well-known dry field farming technique in CFT. This method grows two crops in one year or three crops in two years, sowing barley and wheat in the fall and using the roots of winter crops in a system of crop rotation.[5]

The evidence that CFT emphasized sowing methods can be seen in the outline of its structure, which (excluding the foreword and appendix) consists of 11 chapters of various kinds of rice, legumes, grains, and other crops, the titles of which all ending in the character for seed are the core techniques presented in CFT. Being consistently concise in its other methods of prepping the seeds, plowing land, and sowing, the book was titled "Concise Farming Talk (*Nongsa chiksŏl*)." An interesting point about CFT is whether it is based on the northern method of dry farming or on the southern method of wet farming.

The dominant mode of thought in current scholarship is that King Sejong compiled CFT in order to disseminate the advanced farming techniques of the three southern provinces, especially Chŏlla Province to the northern provinces of Hamgyŏng and P'yŏngan. However, this book argues that this view is flawed, as the main content of CFT addresses techniques that were based on the mountainous areas and dry fields found throughout most of the Korean Peninsula. This perhaps is most evident in the case of the high praise by Takeda Shōchishiro for the "dry rice farming method" of P'yŏngan Province and the "three crops in two years method" of Hwanghae Province as cutting-edge farming techniques.

Takeda discovered that the origin of these techniques lay in CFT, which were core techniques also mentioned alongside with double-cropping. Takeda also discovered that 50% of the farmland of P'yŏngan Province, amounting to about 50,000 hectares, combined wet and dry

---

[5] Wi Ŭnsuk (1990, pp. 1–26).

farming methods. These so-called dry rice (*kŏndo*⁶) were grown in these and other provinces where drylands were much more abundant than wetlands, which were sown with dry farming techniques and raised with wet farming techniques, and could be used with whatever technique was appropriate to the climate.

As rain usually did not fall during the first 10–20 days of the fifth lunar month throughout the Korean Peninsula when planting rice, it is believed that this type of "dry rice" was developed in P'yŏngan Province by sowing them in dry fields, which were then transferred to paddies during the heavy rains in the rainy season the seventh lunar month.⁷

Takeda also praised the "three crops in two years method" as a stroke of genius in using farmland,⁸ further emphasizing that the method could not exist without the sequence of growing barley, legumes, and millet. The barley winter crop was the main focus of this method, and as intercropping and companion cropping were also possible with this method, large and wide embankments were built in which barely was planted in between the embankments and furrows to shield them from the cold winter winds and to irrigate them with water.

In contrast, legume crops were sown on top of the embankments as they were resistant to drought in their early stages of growth. Thus, the intercropping of barley and legumes, wherein the former needed shade and the latter needed sunlight, was the perfect match. If legumes were planted on the embankments, then water did not stagnate even during the rainy season and the leaves flourished, shading the barley in the furrows. The inclusion of millet into this method was because it was a crop that could be sown anytime and grew quickly despite barrenness of the land and receiving little fertilizer.⁹

These methods were similar to the "dry farming" techniques used in Europe since the 1880s, while combining intensive land use with wet fields, and what is most interesting is that a technique appearing in Europe in the late nineteenth century was already recognized for its importance by the state and published in Korea in the fifteenth century. The "dry rice farming method" was especially difficult to pull off as there

---

⁶ 乾稻.
⁷ In-Taek Oh (2003, pp. 65–78).
⁸ Takeda Shōchishiro (1929, p. 862).
⁹ Takeda Shōchishiro (1929, p. 863).

was a drought period of approximately 60–70 days from the fifth to seventh lunar months despite sowing barley which naturally demanded water in order to grow. In addition, another point worthy of attention is the fact that the farming implements used for this technique were made of wood and small in size.

However, the dominant view held in Korean academia completely contradicts the nature of the "dry rice farming method" and "three crops in two years method," arguing that CFT was published in order to disseminate the wet field farming developed in Chŏlla, Kyŏngsang, and Ch'ungch'ŏng Provinces to the less developed farmland of P'yŏngan and Hamgyŏng Provinces. However, the foreword in CFT clearly states that the knowledge of advanced farming techniques in all the provinces was acquired through multiple trials, with no evidence of advanced or less developed regions. As rational farming methods native to Korea worthy of international recognition, the "dry rice farming method" of P'yŏngan Province and the "three crops in two years method" of Hwanghae Province should rather be judged as among the most advanced farming methods.

Thus, this book claims that King Sejong sought to standardize the wisdom and experience of the dry field farming developed by P'yŏngan and Hamgyŏng farmers and the wet field farming developed by Chŏlla and Kyŏngsang farmers in a national language and also combine the two methods. The evidence in support of the compilation of CFT as the opportunity for inventing the national system of communication, *hangŭl*, can be found in the experiences of the sowing methods of early-sowing rice varieties in the northern and southern border regions.

Here, we can see King Sejong's innovative idea to exchange the early-sowing rice varieties planted in the southern Chŏlla, Kyŏngsang, and Ch'ungch'ŏng Provinces with those of the northern P'yŏngan and Hamgyŏng Provinces to discover the best sowing periods in each region in order to develop early-sowing rice varieties. Between the compilation of CFT in 1429 and invention of *hangŭl* in 1446, King Sejong dispatched Pak Kŭn of P'yŏngan in 1438 and also commanded him to survey the migrations of southerners in Chŏlla, Kyŏngsang, and Ch'ungch'ŏng Provinces. Pak Kŭn then went to each village in the southern provinces and demanded that 50 *sŏk* of early-sowing rice seed grain be assigned to each village and also exchanged with their own seed. In particular, he took back 10 *sŏk* of seed to Yŏyŏn and Kanggye, and five *sŏk* of seed to *Chasŏng*, all villages in the north, and petitioned King

Sejong to have the magistrates of each village sow the seeds at the appropriate time in order to test them.[10]

The governors of all eight provinces were made to tour all 337 counties and districts and collect empirical records that had long stood the test of time for collation in the capital, from which these were all synthesized and compiled as CFT. King Sejong sought to soothe relations with Ming China by exporting early-sowing rice while expanding the northern territories of P'yŏngan and Hamgyŏng Provinces from Koryŏ's boundaries to where they are today. What is interesting here is that the expansion of the northern territories is also intimately tied with the project of developing new varieties of early-sowing rice. King Sejong ordered officials in the northern regions that 25 sŏm of early-sowing rice seed be sown as soon as the ice melted, *ŏromgŏtki*[11] and *kuhwangdoeori*,[12] as written in CFT. In particular, the *ŏrŭmgŏtki* and *kuhwangdoeori* varieties, which had Korean names, were taken from the most northern reaches of Yŏyŏn and Kanggye and sown in every region.

Taking the early-sowing varieties grown in the coldest areas of the country and planting them throughout the entire country to determine their appropriate sowing periods was a truly innovative experiment. In other words, sowing early-sowing rice varieties from the north in Chŏlla and Kyŏngsang Provinces where the ice melted first was an experiment of innovation to invention.

Therefore, this invention of sowing and growing techniques of early-sowing rice varieties during the compilation of CFT is in fact a variety that is native to Korea, and the invention of *hangŭl* is also linked to this issue. As the early-sowing rice varieties in CFT were developed in regions outside of the Sino-literary sphere and to do away with the inconvenience of borrowing Chinese characters to fulfill domestic demand for the grain, it is likely that King Sejong decided to develop a new alphabet to disseminate knowledge of these native varieties in order to distinguish them from those in the Sino-literary sphere and for the accumulation and communication of information specific to Korea (Fig. 5.1, Tables 5.1 and 5.2).

---

[10] Annals of King Sejong, 20/04/04 1431.

[11] 氷析稻 어롬것기.

[12] 救荒狄所里 구황되오리.

5 DROUGHT: ENDURING AND LEGUMINOUS PLANTS SCIENCE 63

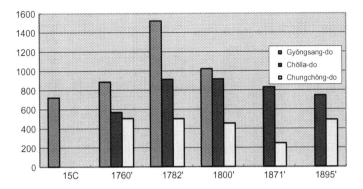

Fig. 5.1 Number of irrigation facilities in southern area (1470–1900) (*Source* Miyajima Hiroshi [1980] and S. H. Jun [1998])

Table 5.1 Rainfall in Chosŏn (1771–1834) (unit: mm)

	Jan	Feb	Mar	Apr	May	Jun	Jul	Aug	Sep	Oct	Nov	Dec	Total
1771'	10	0	91	17	50	273	108	39	37	25	31	0	681
1772'	10	0	29	0	35	8	0	197	0	19	29	2	329
1773'	0	6	52	37	2	97	188	149	2	37	12	0	582
1774'	0	0	2	162	15	25	137	174	62	31	10	10	628
1775'	10	0	6	116	19	137	151	0	23	4	25	50	541
1776'	6	0	22	79	70	17	389	37	43	25	0	48	736
1777'	0	0	15	6	50	8	21	162	81	56	75	0	474
1778'	0	33	0	17	62	122	259	190	66	25	4	0	778
1779'	0	0	99	64	31	344	99	159	41	97	52	10	996
1780'	2	4	0	68	37	77	186	122	122	12	39	0	669
1781'	6	15	46	37	54	269	385	219	155	4	15	23	1228
1782'	0	4	8	4	25	39	337	180	97	10	17	48	769
1783'	0	0	2	54	41	126	95	395	60	89	6	0	868
1784'	0	62	8	101	73	157	375	112	435	95	85	8	1511
1785'	0	0	8	44	68	89	251	41	81	97	19	8	706
1786'	0	0	10	31	93	77	379	195	33	8	2	19	847
1787'	0	0	47	54	17	414	745	335	294	15	37	0	1958
1788'	41	19	50	27	91	89	410	85	236	52	15	0	1115
1789'	0	0	29	213	66	209	416	306	52	56	21	23	1391
1790'	0	0	35	33	114	110	354	95	19	0	15	0	775
1791'	31	0	17	17	143	188	373	648	124	118	52	83	1794
1792'	0	0	27	44	101	304	524	246	197	21	15	0	1479
1793'	0	0	23	95	95	201	253	39	157	50	31	17	961

(continued)

Table 5.1 (continued)

	Jan	Feb	Mar	Apr	May	Jun	Jul	Aug	Sep	Oct	Nov	Dec	Total
1794'	27	6	17	39	116	135	141	170	147	46	66	19	929
1795'	2	6	27	17	60	110	290	151	23	10	41	0	737
1796'	0	4	135	75	41	313	286	244	62	89	93	0	1342
1797'	6	0	64	79	0	149	271	215	116	6	27	0	933
1798'	0	23	27	70	95	29	453	130	170	12	64	101	1174
1799'	17	2	10	64	43	110	513	284	17	52	46	12	1170
1800'	8	0	19	172	60	52	534	358	236	93	27	12	1571
1801'	0	39	4	43	77	77	248	277	77	23	39	6	910
1802'	12	0	64	97	110	219	340	294	68	33	79	0	1316
1803'	12	0	58	64	37	66	304	95	97	104	81	0	918
1804'	0	0	8	89	77	33	638	344	44	27	68	0	1328
1805'	0	12	159	89	106	170	261	294	182	91	104	21	1489
1806'	6	21	70	234	253	352	64	294	217	77	85	10	1683
1807'	0	0	15	39	108	157	188	462	35	52	35	8	1099
1808'	0	0	29	89	46	114	476	168	41	56	68	4	1091
1809'	10	0	97	31	79	52	282	188	157	12	35	0	943
1810'	0	6	0	12	168	25	586	536	261	91	31	0	1716
1811'	0	0	99	31	8	116	580	350	81	73	35	12	1385
1812'	0	79	99	157	15	110	213	50	31	114	33	0	901
1813'	0	0	122	6	37	118	418	373	50	48	23	19	1214
1814'	4	4	50	4	35	50	211	619	97	64	35	10	1183
1815'	0	0	46	39	25	157	364	385	155	52	10	0	1233
1816'	0	52	10	101	95	81	809	544	77	35	66	0	1870
1817'	0	0	52	108	60	89	580	646	54	12	48	25	1674
1818'	0	8	6	48	162	35	443	369	155	106	70	12	1414
1819'	0	0	60	4	31	118	366	205	397	12	46	27	1266
1820'	0	101	6	77	97	178	505	58	164	25	41	0	1252
1821'	0	41	10	119	81	232	**1184**	**681**	178	110	29	6	2671
1822'	0	0	95	46	87	155	99	151	93	27	44	12	809
1823'	4	31	79	17	91	151	331	128	128	33	54	12	1059
1824'	0	21	39	46	112	147	480	284	44	126	83	21	1403
1825'	0	0	0	60	54	39	170	340	97	110	10	8	888
1826'	0	19	6	39	128	271	350	278	48	6		8	1153
1827'	0	0	37	93	253	246	238	307	261	46	43	31	1555
1828'	75	0	37	31	41	110	404	588	263	6	62	27	1644
1829'	0	0	60	73	114	79	226	75	209	120	8	8	972
1830'	0	0	12	110	21	58	453	402	56	308	10	8	1438
1831'	0	23	52	58	137	0	91	186	120	58	31	0	756
1832'	15	10	0	110	17	31	**1348**	333	238	8	79	35	2224
1833'	0	0	12	58	87	85	480	911	54	19	50	44	1800
1834'	0	0	6	12	104	106	203	128	251	97	8	10	925

Table 5.2 Classification Standard of Rainfall for Table 5.1

Climatic zone	Annual rainfall (mm)	Wet period (month)	Vegetation	Land use (major crops)
Desert	Less than 100	0'–3'	Little or no vegetation	Hunters and gatherers, nomadic pastoralists, sedentary irrigators around oases, no rainfed agriculture
Arid	100–400	1'–3'	Some scrubs, some grassland	Extensive grazing (nomadic pastoralists), some millet and sorghum under flood irrigation in moist depressions
Semi-arid	400–600	3'–4'	Scrubs & bushes, grassland	Both nomadic pastoralists and cultivators. Mainly millet and sorghum, also short cycle cowpea, phaseolus beans and groundnuts. No fodder or sown pasture. In cooler parts maize
Sub-humid	600–1200	4'–6'	Bushes to woodland, grassland	Traditional nomadic pastoralists in dry season and drought years. Crops grown by settlers: millet, sorghum, maize, groundnuts; also cassava, cowpeas, cotton, sweet potatoes, tobacco, rainfed rice, soybean, mango, cashewnuts. Fodder and sown pasture possible
Moist sub-humid	1200–1500	6'–9'	Forest and woodland	Transition zone for agriculture: too wet for seasonal crops, too dry for tree crops. Tropics: maize, cassava; also yams, bananas, pineapple, sugarcane and rice. Winter rainfall areas and East African highlands: wheat and barley
Humid	More than 1500	9'–12'	Tropical rain forest	Tree crops: oilpalm, rubber, cacao; shifting cultivation based on root crops (yams, cassava, etc.). Also some sorghum, maize, banana, sugarcane, rice. Some tropical hard woods

Source The International Support Programme for irrigation Water Management, Land and Water Development Division, Food and Agriculture Organization (FAO 1986)

REFERENCES

F. H. King. *Farmers of Forty Centuries, or Permanent Agriculture in China, Korea and Japan.* Madison, 1911.

In-Taek Oh. The Making of Dry Farming Area on Wet Field and the Characteristics of the Dry Farming System in the 18th and 19th Centuries. *Journal of Agricultural History*, Vol. 2, No. 2 (Korea Agricultural History Association), pp. 65–78, 2003.

Ja-Ock Guh and Yong In Kuk. Weeding Hypothesis on Direct Seeding Rice Field as Applied by the Old Firing and Water Dressing Method. *Korean Journal of Weed Science*, Vol. 31, No. 1, pp. 1–7, 2011.

Jun Seong Ho. *A History of Rice Price in Late Chosŏn: 1725–1875.* Ph. D. Dissertation. Sung Kyun Kwan University (『조선후기 米價史 연구: 1725–1875』). 1998.

Jun Seong Ho and Evelyn Ruiz Gamarra. A Story of Globally Important Agricultural Wisdom in the 15th Century Chosŏn Korea. *Anthropology*, Vol. 6, No. 2, pp. 1–6, 2018.

Miyajima Hiroshi (宮嶋博史), 朝鮮農業史における15世紀朝鮮史叢, Vol. 3, pp. 3–83, June 1980.

R. Bean, B. W. Olesen, and K. W. Kim. History of Radiant Heating & Cooling Systems: Part 1. *ASHRAE Journal*, Vol. 14, pp. 40–47, 2010.

Takahashi Noboru (高橋昇). Chōsen hantō no nōhō to nōmin (朝鮮半島の農法と農民). Edited by Kuiinuma, Jirō (飯沼二郎), Takahashi, Kōshirō (高橋甲四郎), and Miyajima, Hiroshi (宮嶋博史). Tokyo: Miraisha (未來社), 1998. Reprint of 1933–1937.

Takeda Shōchishiro. (武川統七郎) 實驗麥作新說 Tokyo (東京) Meibundo (明文堂), 1929.

Wi Ŭnsuk. Koryo Period Farming Techniques and Productivity Research (Koryŏ sidae nongŏp kisul kwa saengsanyŏk yŏngu). *Kuksagwan Nonŏp*, Vol. 17, pp. 1–26, 1990.

CHAPTER 6

The Organization of CFT

The Food Agriculture Organization of the United Nations has recognized around the world a few locally adapted and complex agricultural systems that have enabled communities to enjoy food security, combining social, cultural, and ecological aspects into techniques and practices that have stood the test of time, resulting in resilient ecosystems and cultural heritage for people of our times. These are denominated as "GIAHS." A report of 2011 states:

> The existence of numerous GIAHS around the world testifies to the inventiveness and ingenuity of people in their use and management of finite resources, biodiversity, ecosystem dynamics, and ingenious use of physical attributes of the landscape, codified in traditional but evolving knowledge, practices and technologies. Whether recognized or not by the scientific community, these ancestral agricultural systems constitute the foundation for contemporary and future agricultural innovations and technologies.[1]

CFT was not only used continuously as the basic instruction manual for state agricultural policy during the five-hundred-year-long Chosŏn dynasty, but also became the basis in the compilation of agricultural texts for scholars throughout the late Chosŏn dynasty after the Japanese invasions of the 1590s. As an instruction manual based on wet field and dry

[1] Koohafkan and Altieri, Food and Agriculture Organization of the United Nations (2011).

field farming techniques, CFT is intimately linked with the state agricultural policy of the Chosŏn dynasty.

The publication of CFT is an important milestone in strengthening the new state based on farming households during fifteenth-century Korea. CFT emphasizes long-term environmental and social sustainability, correlated with the management of soil, water, and biological resources so that rural people can also use said resources. To be socially sustainable, farming must improve nutrition and income in ways that it may be prosperous and encourage local self-reliance and a rational distribution of resources. This means farming that uses local resources available to all households; these resources include indigenous farming techniques and other crops indigenous.

CFT is organized into three parts: Part I is a preface giving an overview of farming and background information regarding the publication of CFT; Part II is the main body composed of eleven chapters. Chapter 9 is about preparing the seed grain, Chapter 10 discusses how to plow using paired oxen, Chapter 10 is about preparing the soil, and Chapter 11 contains information on planting hemp. Chapter 12 is about cultivating rice (with a supplemental section on upland rice) and consists of three main techniques for cultivation and planting: The first one is wet farming, the second is dry farming, and the third is transplanting. Chapter 12 also includes two methods which are not listed in the original version of CFT but do appear in the seventeenth-century CFH. Chapter 13 is about cultivating Proso/Foxtail Millet (including *Chŏmmulgok Foxtail Millet*, *Ch'ŏngnyang Foxtail Millet*, and Sorghum). Chapter 14 is about growing glutinous millet (including kangjik). Chapter 15 covers growing soybeans, red beans, and mung beans. Chapter 16 discusses cultivating barley and wheat (including ch'unmo). Chapter 17 describes growing sesame (known locally as Chinimja). Chapter 18 summarizes growing buckwheat (known locally as mokmaek). The last part reviews the glossary.

All this compiled knowledge is a rich source of information that now becomes available thanks to the initiative of those who understood that adaptation to one's environment conditions is the key to survive and that knowledge that concerns something as basic as agriculture, needed for subsistence of the people, needs to be widespread since it is the kind of practical information that needs to be put to use and tested instead of remaining in books just as theories. Some of the techniques native to Korea's geography described in CFT could be rescued and put to use in combination with modern agriculture to make the most of the resources that can be found on the Korean Peninsula, especially North Korea.

As Korea is a country with a rich agricultural background, we can notice the similarities that early-modern agriculture in Korea and India, Vietnam and Inca shared when trying to make the most of mountainous lands, subsisting and living in harmony with their natural environments.

This link can be found in the fact that the arable land of the 336 counties and districts of the eight provinces of fifteenth-century Chosŏn was classified into wet fields and dry fields, the scales and proportions of which were surveyed and recorded in the *GAVK* (Sejong sillok chiriji).[2] CFT was the basic instruction manual of state agricultural policy and also an instruction manual on compiling farming texts for later agricultural scholars. For example, the chapter on farm management in *Hanjŏngnok*[3] by Hŏ Kyun (1569–1618), the mid-Chosŏn writer famous for *The Tale of Hong Kildong*, contains a summary of CFT. Later, in the seventeenth and eighteenth centuries, the same chapter on farming in *Sallim kyŏngje*[4] by Hong Mansŏn (1643–1715) also bases itself on the contents of CFT. In addition, it can also be found in the same location in the *Revised and Augmented Sallim kyŏngje*[5] written by Yu Chungrim (1705–1771) in 1776. CFT is also the foundation of *Imwŏn kyŏngjeji*[6] written by Sŏ Yugu (1764–1845) in the mid-nineteenth century.

CFT became known internationally in the late nineteenth century and Japanese colonial period through a French bibliographic scholar and Japanese agricultural scholar, respectively. In the late nineteenth century, the French bibliographic scholar Maurice Courant (1865–1935) compiled *Bibliographie coréenne* as a three-volume set in 1894 as a result of having intensively purchased and researched Korean texts that were printed in the Koryŏ and Chosŏn periods while he was in Korea as secretary to the French legation from 1890 to 1892. CFT appears as entry 2554 in Courant's bibliography and is introduced as a text compiled by royal command through surveying farmers throughout the eight provinces.[7]

[2] 世宗實錄地理志.
[3] 閑情錄.
[4] 山林經濟.
[5] 增補山林經濟.
[6] 林園經濟志.
[7] Maurice Courant (1936, pp. 101–107).

During the Japanese colonial period, Japanese agricultural scholar Takahashi Noboru (1892–1946) conducted on-site surveys and studied old farming texts in his research on Chosŏn's agricultural history. In June 1919, he was appointed to the Japanese Governor-General's Industrial Model Farm (Experimental Farm) in Suwŏn and he surveyed farming techniques throughout Korea while he stayed in the country for twenty-seven years until the end of the Second World War. So impressed was he by the intensive farming methods practiced by Koreans that he praised them as advanced technologies that were unimaginable in Europe and the USA, and his mention of CFT in a literary source makes him as the most conscientious Japanese agricultural scholar during the Japanese colonial period.[8]

Although CFT is the oldest farming text in Korea containing techniques that were impressive not only during its compilation in the fifteenth century but even up until the twentieth century, the original copy compiled by order of King Sejong in 1429 has not been found. The extant copies dating from before and after the Japanese invasions of the 1590s differ vastly. The edition prior to the Japanese invasions was granted to local officials from the central government in 1581, and the edition after the Japanese invasions was compiled in 1655 by Kongju magistrate Sin Sok as part of *Compilation for Farmers* (*Nongga chipsŏng*, 農家集成, CFH) which contained CFT, *Miscellanies on Kŭmyang District* (Kumyang chapnok 衿陽雜錄, MKD), and *Compiled Essential Excerpts on the Four Seasons* (Sasi ch'anyoch'o 四時纂要抄, CEF).

The oldest edition of CFT prior to the Japanese invasions is thought to be in Japan. According to Miyajima Hiroshi, Japan has five copies of CFT, two of which are in the National Diet Library, two in the Cabinet Library, and one in Osaka's Takeda Pharmaceutical Company. Of these, the copy in the National Diet Library was printed in the ninth year of the Wanli Emperor in 1581 and granted to Ch'unch'ŏn magistrate Pak Sŭngim (1517–1586). Pak's copy is thought to have been granted from the central government when he took office as magistrate of Ch'unch'ŏn in 1581. Much of the content in the edition stored in the Kyujanggak Archives of Seoul National University is missing in comparison with the edition in CFF compiled by Sin Sok in the second year of King Hyojong's reign in 1661. The edition of CFT translated into Japanese

---

[8]Takahashi Noboru (1998, p. 95).

by Miyajima Hiroshi is the same as that held in Kyujanggak. The original text of this English and Korean translation of CFT is based on the 1581 edition granted to Ch'unch'ŏn magistrate Pak Sŭngim and the 1655 edition held in the National Library.

REFERENCES

Maurice Courant. Introduction to the Bibliographie Coreenne. *Transactions of the Korea Branch of the Royal Asiatic Society*, Vol. 25, pp. 1–100, 1936.
Trollope Mark Napier, Book Production and Printing in Corea. *Transactions of the Korea Branch of the Royal Asiatic Society* Vol. 25, pp. 101–107, 1936.
P. Koohafkan and M. A. Altieri. *Globally Important Agricultural Heritage Systems. A Legacy for the Future*. Rome: Food and Agriculture Organization of the United Nations, 2011.
Takahashi Noboru. *The Farmers and Farming Techniques of the Korean Peninsula* (Chosŏnbando ŭi nongbŏp kwa nongmin). Minsokwŏn, 1998.

CHAPTER 7

Conclusion

Through the introduction and creation of the English translation of CFT, we have learned through its contents the richness and abundance of agricultural knowledge in Korea, dating from centuries ago when the main concern of the dynasty was to guarantee a constant supply of crops that could be cultivated using techniques that were familiar and that could solve problems unique to the geographic conditions of this lands. In this sense, the compilation of this valuable knowledge speaks of a will to preserve the agricultural culture of its people looking to pass it on to future generations that could build on it.

The existence of CFT in fifteenth-century Korea testifies to the inventiveness and ingenuity of Korean farmers in their use and management of limited resources, biodiversity, ecosystem dynamics, and ingenious use of physiognomies of the Korean topography, categorized for traditional knowledge, practices, and technologies.

Whether recognized or not by the scientific community, these ancestral agricultural systems constitute the foundation for contemporary and future agricultural innovations and technologies. Their cultural, ecological, and agricultural diversity is still evident in many parts of the world, maintained as unique systems of agriculture. Through a remarkable process of coevolution of humankind and nature, GIAHS have emerged over centuries of cultural and biological interactions and synergies, representing the accumulated experiences of rural people.

Nowadays, the risk of increasing surface ozone on our planet represents a potential threat to the environment and affects everyone all around the world. Therefore, we are faced with the need for a more effective strategy to improve agricultural production without the environmental damage associated with conventional methods of increasing crop yields.

CFT suggests an optimistic scenario for the future and against the growing threat the climate change poses to global food security. The knowledge of CFT can contribute to reduce surface ozone concentrations thus providing an excellent opportunity to increase global grain yields without the environmental degradation associated with organic land cultivation.[1]

Through a comparative analysis of the compilation of farming texts from the fifteenth century and their recorded grain varieties, starting with CEA imported from China during King Taejong's reign, CFT compiled during King Sejong's reign, and MKD, we have examined the state's management systems in compiling and its relative significance.

This book has also argued that CFT was the center of the Imitation-Innovation-Invention development path, starting with imitating CEA, innovating with CFT in order to adapt to the differences in Korean topography (1419–1429), the expansion of Hamgil Province and metal typography (1434), the invention and installation of rain measures (1442), the invention and promulgation of *hangŭl* (1443 and 1446, respectively), and the labeling of grains in *hangŭl* in MKD (1492), all of which were part of the innovation-invention stage. The results of this study call for questioning the current trend of focusing on agricultural farming methods on the fifteenth-century farming texts, which mainly focus on distinguishing between Chinese farming methods such as Huabei-based crop rotation and Jiangnan-based paddy fields, labeling the imported version of CEA during King Taejong's reign as supporting the former and King Sejong's CFT as supporting the latter. The research here is broadly divided into two positions.

The first position views these texts as adopting the farming methods of the three southern provinces, Chŏlla, Ch'ungch'ŏng, and Kyŏngsang Provinces, as the basis for spreading advanced agricultural methods to the north's Hamgyŏng and P'yŏngyang Provinces. Landowners and wealthy farmers are regarded as the agents of agricultural productivity, with the extensive farming opening the path for business operations nationwide.

---

[1] Shiri Avnery et al. (2011, p. 2297).

7 CONCLUSION

The other position is that these texts were scientific technologies that led to the adoption of the crop rotation method of Hwanghae Province in areas with paddy fields, leading to intensive small-scale farming.

This study offers an opinion differing from the previous literature by focusing on the specific techniques described in CFT and the compilation processes of CFT and MKD in the fifteenth century. First, it argues that the core of fifteenth-century farming techniques was growing techniques mentioned in CFT discovered in the process of importing from abroad rice varieties and adapting them to Korea's topography. As these growing techniques were discovered from the trials and experiences of farmers from all over the country, this suggests that there is more to the farming techniques rather than the argument in prior studies that the southern regions had more advanced farming techniques than the northern regions.

Next, by highlighting the fact that the planting techniques and grain labels developed by CFT were used to plant grains in infertile lands, it suggests that these techniques could be applied by both petty and wealthy farmers for extensive or intensive farming, which differs from the analysis that intensive farming was practiced only by farmers with small landholdings. Finally, it showed how the limits of *idu* in translating the grain labels that were the focus of growing techniques invoked the necessity of inventing *hangŭl*, depicting the link between the development of agricultural science and the invention of *hangŭl* during the reign of King Sejong.

Examining Korea's native rice varieties listed in CFT shows us how significant of an effect the text had in recording Korea's agricultural traditions through the written word, which is a confluence of a cognitive process and socioeconomic institutions, something unimaginable in an oral culture. Thus, the effect of writing in raising the cognitive abilities of the entire population can be perceived in the grain labels of CFT and the systemic and standardized collection of farmers' knowledge which resulted in achievements that produced a continuity of knowledge and promoted standardization and preservation of that knowledge.

CFT is the ideal text to understand the nature of the circulation of useful information and productive knowledge possessed by farmers. Thus, the groundbreaking achievement of the fifteenth century was CFT furnishing a system of gathering useful knowledge upon a phonological foundation. As it is widely known, King Sejong invented *hangŭl* in order to resolve the problem of miscommunication and dichotomy between the oral and written languages of Korea. The motivation for its invention was previously already laid out during the compilation of CFT.[2]

CFT was a model of state administration, shows the state's strong tendency to promote the knowledge economy. The transition from the ephemerality of oral culture to the permanence of written culture substituted the non-permanence and non-attributability of the former for permanence and attributability. King Sejong invented *hangŭl* based on CFT's underlying intention to lexically archive for the future productive and useful knowledge passed down orally from generation to generation in an agricultural society. CFT overcame the limits of the imitation stage of importing and translating the agricultural science and techniques of Huabei, China, based on the intellectual elite's Chinese characters, opening a new stage of innovation and invention administered by the state. If King Sejong's scientific knowledge policy of depending on what King Taejong had imported was based on the "trickle down theory," then the significance of a technical text to systemically standardize the knowledge of farmers in every province who had based their agricultural practice on knowledge accumulated over thousands of years was much greater than the former's. The invention of *hangŭl* provided the crucial juncture which dissolved the dichotomy between the knowledge accumulated by farmers and the state's language system and brought them together. CFT's overcoming of the limits of time and space by accumulating past and present information in order to rationally prepare for the future on the order of the entire country is deeply connected with the invention of *hangŭl*.

REFERENCES

F. Niyi Akinnaso. The Consequences of Literacy in Pragmatic and Theoretical Perspectives. *Anthropology & Education Quarterly*, Vol. 12, No. 3, pp. 163–200, 1981.

Shiri Avnerya, Denise L. Mauzerallb, Junfeng Liuc, and Larry W. Horowitzc. Global Crop Yield Reductions Due to Surface Ozone Exposure: 2. Year 2030 Potential Crop Production Losses and Economic Damage Under Two Scenarios of O3 Pollution. *Atmospheric Environment*, Vol. 45, No. 13, pp. 2297–2309, April 2011.

---

[2] F. Niyi Akinnaso (1981, pp. 163–200).

PART II

English Translation of Concise Farming Talk (Nongsa chiksŏl)

EXPLANATORY NOTE

- This document uses the lunar month system with references to some of the 24 solar terms. All references to years or months are referring to the lunar system. Furthermore, a lunar month is divided into three parts, called upper, middle, and lower *sun*, which are comprised of 10 days each. This Sino-Korean word "*sun*" has been translated as "week" in this text because it can easily be confused with the English word sun. Upper, middle, and lower have been translated as first, second, and third.
- Original annotations (those in the source text) are marked in square brackets.
- Words added by the translators to aid in conveying the meaning are marked in parenthesis.
- Annotations by the translators are included via endnotes.
- The English translation here is based on the edition that was compiled in 1655 by *Sin Sok* as part of CFH which contained three books CFT, MKD, and CEF. The edition preserved in the *Jangseogak* Archives of the Academy of Korean Studies (AKS) and the National Library of Korea (NLK). We have a permission for copyright from AKS.

CHAPTER 8

Preface

Regulator-General Chŏng Ch'o[1] and others were ordered to compile *Concise Theory of Farming*. The preface reads:
Farming is the great foundation of all states under Heaven. Since the ancient times, there has been no sage king who did not commit himself to farming. In the sage King Shun's[2] order to his nine ministers and twelve governors, he first said:

Crop yields! They depend entirely on timing.

Indeed, as they are used as offerings in sacrificial rites and sustenance, they must not be ignored.
As your subject reverently recalls, the late King Taejong[3] once ordered his ministers to copy ancient texts[4] on farming and select the essence, attach commentary in the common language, carve the woodblocks, print them out, distribute the copies, and enlighten the people and have them focus on the fundamental task of farming. My Lord, Your Majesty (King Sejong[5]),

---

[1] Civil official of Chosŏn, ?–1434, of the Hadong Chŏng clan.
[2] A legendary leader of ancient China said to have reigned 2294 and 2184 BCE.
[3] The third king of the Chosŏn dynasty, r. 1400–1418; Father of King Sejong, the king to whom this preface is addressed.
[4] The ancient Chinese agricultural texts such as Fàn shèng zhī shū from the Hàn, Qimin Yaoshu from the Northern Wei.
[5] The fourth king of the Chosŏn dynasty, r. 1418–1450.

inherited the grand design for governing from your illustrious predecessor (i.e., Taejong), devoting yourself even more to the people's affairs.

The natural features vary across the country. Therefore, each region has its own way of sowing and cultivating, and the old farming texts should not be blindly followed. And then, the governors of all provinces were ordered to go around the counties and districts, call on the seasoned farmers, and listen carefully to their tried and true experiences on the land. Furthermore (Your Majesty) ordered your subject (Chŏng) Ch'o to complete the job of adding explanations. Next your subject (Chŏng Cho), along with Royal Genealogist Pyŏn Hyomun,[6] revised separate accounts in reference to other sources, eliminated the redundancies, selected the essentials, and completed a single volume called *Concise Farming Talk*.

[This text] does not cover other topics, such as horticulture and sericulture. The priority is on conciseness and straightforwardness, so that people from rural areas can clearly understand it without effort. (The order) for printing has been already handed down to the Bureau of Typecasting[7] and several few copies shall be printed for dispersal throughout the country. This will guide the people and enrich their livelihoods; thereby, the benefits shall extend to every household and provide for all the people.

Your subject pondered over the poetry of Zhou[8] and (concluded that) the Zhou ruling house[9] based the state on farming and thus it lasted over eight hundred years. Now Your Majesty's gracious nurturing of our people and long-held concern about the state, how is this standard not the same with that of Houji[10] and King Cheng[11] of Zhou? Though this book is small, its benefits cannot be expressed in words!

---

[6] Civil official of Chosŏn, 1395–?, of the Ch'ogye Pyŏn clan.

[7] Established first in 1403; the copper type made at that time was called *kyemi* type (after the cyclical year designation for 1403).

[8] Referring to the *Classic of Poetry*.

[9] The Zhou dynasty of China lasted from 1046 to 314 BCE.

[10] A legendary agricultural hero in the East Asia introducing millet to humanity during the time of the Xia dynasty. Millet was the original staple grain of northern East Asia, prior to the introduction of wheat. The name means Lord of Millet.

[11] The second king of the Zhou dynasty, r. 1042–1021 BCE.

CHAPTER 9

Preparing the Seeds

Collect seeds of the nine crops[1] and select those that are healthy, unmixed, and not damp. [Damp seeds refer to those that are slightly wet and smelly. If the seed is not healthy, the next year's yield will also be unhealthy. The embryo of the aforementioned seed will already be diseased. If the early- and late-sowing varieties are mixed, they will grow at different paces. If the seeds are damp, they will not germinate, and even if they do, they will not ripen.]

First, winnowing[2] the seeds and remove the chaff.[3] Then, submerge them in water, remove those which float, and sieve to get them from the water. Then, place (the seeds) under the sun until they are perfectly dry. Store them securely in a *hoch'ŏn*.[4] [Its common name is *pinsŏm*. If there is even a little moisture, most of the seeds will become damp.]

- If you want to know which seeds among the nine grains will be suitable for the following year, take one *toe*[5] of seeds per each of the nine grains, put them in hemp sacks, and bury (the sacks) inside

---

[1] The "nine grains" refers to the basic crops which were cultivated. Though called the nine "grains," the list includes hemp, as well.

[2] See Appendix B, No. I.

[3] The North Korean translation (1957) translates this not as chaff, but as empty heads of grain.

[4] Basket made of rice straw and bamboo.

[5] One toe is about 0.6 liters.

© The Author(s) 2019
S. H. Jun, *Agriculture and Korean Economic History*,
https://doi.org/10.1007/978-981-32-9319-9_9

of a storage pit. [Do not allow people to sit or lie on it.] After fifty days, open the storage pit, take out the sacks, and examine them. Those with the most sprouts are suitable for the following year.

As the suitability of farming conditions differs according to the properties of soil of each region, it is necessary to have each village test (which grains are appropriate).

- During the winter months, the seeds should be stored in an earthenware jar or wooden tub, (which is then) buried. It is imperative that (the contents) not freeze.

In the last month of the year, collect a sufficient amount of melted snow, store it to the brim in a *chŏmch'ŏn* [Its common name is *nalgae*.[6]], and cover it thickly. [Ancient texts say snow is the vital force of the five grains.[7]] When it is time for sowing, soak the seeds in the melted snow, take them out, and dry them under the sun. Repeat this process two times.[8]

Alternatively, soak the seeds in a wooden tub[9] filled with urine from the sump on the floor of the cow and horse stable, then take (the seeds) out and dry them under the sun; repeat this process three times.

---

[6] See Appendix B, No. II-2.
[7] Refers to rice, foxtail millet, proso millet, barley, and soybeans.
[8] According to the NLK, it is repeated 3 times.
[9] See Appendix B, No. III.

CHAPTER 10

Plowing the Soil

- Plowing should be done slowly. When done slowly, the soil becomes soft, and the ox toes not tire. Spring and summer plowing should be shallow, and autumn plowing should be deep. For spring plowing, harrow the soil right after it is plowed; for autumn plowing, wait for the soil to dry out and the color turn white, then harrow.
- For dry fields, straw should be spread and burned after the first plowing. The fields will be naturally enriched after plowing again.[1]
- For poor fields, plow and plant mung beans. When they become lush, turn over the soil as is. Then there will be no weeds and no insects, and the barren soil will become fertile. When the soil thaws in the following year, plow once more and then sow.
- For uncultivated land, plow between seventh and eighth months and cover the land with grass. In general, when reclaiming uncultivated land, the first plowing should be deep, and the second plowing should be shallow. [If you first plow deeply and then shallowly, the subsoil is not exposed, making the soil soft and fertile.]

---

[1] The edition held by the NLK adds the following: Generally, planting mung beans is the best method for making fertile fields, and red beans and sesame are the next best method.

CHAPTER 11

Cultivating Hemp

When the soil thaws in the first month, select good fields. If the fields are abundant, rotate them annually. [If (the fields are) rotated annually, then the bark (of the hemp's stem) will be thin, and the space between the joints wide.]

Plow three times lengthwise and three times breadthwise. Spread cow and horse manure (over the field). In the first week[1] of the second month, plow again. [Plowing again in the second week is the second best time, and the third week is the worst time. In the northern regions, the (spring) thaw comes later, and this should be taken into consideration when selecting the best time (for plowing). (The plowing for) all nine grains (should) follow this.]

With a *mokchak*[2] [Its common name is *sohŭlla*.] and a *ch'ŏlch'ip'a*[3] [Its common name is *susuŭm*.], level the soil well, and then evenly and densely tamp it down with your feet.

[1] A lunar month has three weeks of 10 days each.
[2] See Appendix B, No. IV, 4–5; a tool used to finely break apart and then evenly smooth out the soil after plowing. The *sohŭlla* mentioned here is pronounced as *mokchak* (木斫) if made of wood and *ch'ŏlch'ip'a* (鐵齒擺) if made of iron in Chinese characters.
See Kim Gwang-ŏn (1986), *Han'guk Nongchongyŏngcheyŏnguwon*, p. 8; Pak Ho-sŏk and Ahn Sŭng-mo (2001), *Han'guk kunong gigu* [Old Agricultural Implements in Korea], Ŏmungak, p. 90.

[3] See Appendix B, No. 5.

Main agricultural product of the Kitan and the Jurchen.

When sowing seeds, it is also necessary to sow them evenly and densely. [If the tamping and sowing are not done evenly and densely, then the hemp may be too rough or too branchy, therefore not suitable for use.] Drag a *ro*[4] to cover the seeds. [Its common name is *kkŭlgae*. To make it, bind multiple branches of wood; pine branches work best.] On top (of the soil), also spread cow and horse manure.

If there are weeds when the hemp has reached three *chon*,[5] then weed them (with a *hoe*[6]). [Do not weed more than once. The late-sowing varieties can be sowed anytime within ten days before or after the Summer Solstice.[7]]

---

[4] See Appendix B, No. VI.
[5] Three *chon* is approx. 6 cm.
[6] See Appendix B, No. IX.
[7] "Summer Solstice," is the 10th solar term, beginning on June 21 and usually falling in the middle of the fifth lunar month.

CHAPTER 12

Cultivating Rice

Including Upland Rice

There are early-sowing varieties and late-sowing varieties. As for cultivation and sowing methods, there are wet farming [Its common name is *musalmi*.], dry farming [Its common name is *marŭnsami*.], and transplanting seedlings [Its common name is *myojong*.]. The weeding method is generally the same for all varieties.

- (For wet farming of) the early-sowing variety:

After the autumn harvest, choose the most fertile wet fields with an accessible source of water [In general, terraced paddy fields should be irrigated from above and drained below. The best (fields) are those that can be irrigated during droughts and drained during the rain. The second (best) are those where still water collects on the low ground. However, long rains may make the water sludgy and turbid, causing the seedlings to rot. The worst are those on high ground where farming is only possible when it rains.] and plow them.

In the winter months, apply manure (onto the fields). [When the (spring) thaw occurs in the first month, plow the fields and apply manure, or alternatively, bring in new soil.] Then, plow again in the first week of the second month. With a *mokchak* [Its common name is *sohŭlla*.], harrow the soil lengthwise and breadthwise. Then again, with a *ch'ŏlch'ip'a* [Its common name is *susuŭm.*], break up the clods of soil to make it ready (for planting).

Before sowing the seeds, soak them in water. After three days, take them out to drain, put them inside a *hoch'ŏn* [Its common name is *pinsŏm*], and store in a warm place. Frequently open (the *hoch'ŏn*) and check (the seeds), making sure they do not become damp and smelly.

When the sprouts become two *pun*[1] long, place them evenly in the paddies and cover them (with soil) using a *p'allo*[2] [Its common name is *pŏnji.*] or a *p'aro*[3] [Its common name is *milgae.*]. Then, irrigate the fields and keep the birds out (until the seedlings grow).

When the seedlings sprout two leaves, drain the water (from the paddy). After completely removing by hand (the tiny weeds) [The seedlings are fragile so a hoe cannot be used. However, if the water evaporates and the soil firms up, a hoe should be used.] between the seedlings, irrigate again. Drain the water each time before weeding. Once weeding is complete, irrigate it. [While the seedlings are still young and fragile, irrigate lightly, and when the seedlings are mature and strong, irrigate heavily.] If the field has a constant source of water such as a stream, so that it does not dry out even in drought, then every time weeding is completed, drain the water, and expose the base (of the plant) to the sunlight. After two days, restart irrigation [so (the plants) withstand wind and drought].

When the seedlings grow to about half a *ch'ŏk*,[4] weed again with a hoe. [The seedlings are firmly rooted, so using a *hoe* is allowed.] When weeding, use your hands to gently rub the soil surface between the seedlings. Weed up to three or four times. [The growth of the plants depends solely on weeding. Moreover, the early-sowing variety grows quickly by nature, so the slightest delay in weeding is not allowed.] When the plant is about to ripen, drain the water. [If the water remains, it delays the ripening.]

The grain of early-sowing varieties is prone to drop (from the ear), so harvest it as soon as it is ripe.

- For wet farming of late-sowing varieties:

Plow the fields when the (spring) thaw occurs in the first month.

---

[1] One *pun* is approx. 0.2 cm.
[2] See Appendix B, No. VII.
[3] See Appendix B, No. VIII.
[4] One *ch'ŏk* is approx. 20 cm.

As for applying manure and bringing in new soil, follow the same method prescribed for the early-sowing varieties. [If new soil is brought in this year, then apply manure or spread weeds the following year, and alternate them.] If the land is muddy or crumbly, or the subsoil water is cold, then bring in new soil or sod. If the land is infertile and barren, then spread cattle and horse manure and oak stems with leaves [Its common name is kaŭlch'o.].[5] Night soil and silkworm droppings[6] are also good. [But they are difficult to procure in large amounts.]

During the period between the first week of the third month and *Grain in Ear*,[7] plow the fields again (and sow the seeds). [In general, plowing and sowing after *Grain in Ear* brings poor harvest.]

Soaking seeds, sowing seeds, covering seeds, irrigating water, and weeding methods are all the same as for early-sowing varieties. [Weeding three times by the middle of the sixth month is best. Weeding three times by the (end of) the sixth month is the second best. Not doing even this amount of weeding is the worst.]

- If a drought occurs in spring, (thus making) it impossible to practice wet farming, one should practice dry farming. [(In this case), sow only the late-sowing varieties.]

The method is as follows:

After plowing, break the clods with *noemok*.[8] [Its common name is *koŭmp'a*.], and harrow the fields with a *mokchak*. [Its common name is *sohŭlla*.]

After preparing the soil in this way, mix one *mal*[9] of rice seed with one *sŏm*[10] of aged manure or a mixture of urine and ash.

---

[5] In Korea, it is common to bring young leafy oak boughs to the rice fields and use them with green manure with ash. These oak boughs were procured for fuel, fertilizer, and food. The origin of their efficient use comes from the Korean *Ondol* system, which used stoves for both cooking and heating. See Kenneth Pomeranz (2000, p. 46) and F. H. King (1911, p. 142).

[6] Silkworms feed upon the leaves of a species of oak growing on the mountain and hill lands in various parts of Korea. See F. H. King (1911, p. 282).

[7] "Grain in Ear," refers to the 9th solar term, beginning on June 5–6 and usually falling at the beginning of the fifth lunar month.

[8] See Appendix B, No. X.

[9] One *mal* is approx. 6 liters. 15 *mal* is one sŏm.

[10] One *sŏm* is approx. 90 liters.

[Urine and ash fertilizer making method[11]: Dig a small pool outside the cow stable to store urine. Burn stalks, bran, chaff, and the like into ashes and mix it with the urine from the pool.]

Plant (the seeds) using the foot sowing method.[12] (After sowing,) (continue to) keep the birds away [until the seedlings start to grow].

Do not irrigate the field until the seedlings grow enough. If weeds grow, do not cease weeding (with a *hoe*), even if there is a drought and the seedlings wither. [There is an old saying that "A hundred rice plants depend on the head of a *hoe*." Old farmers also said, "Seedlings appreciate a man's efforts (at weeding)."]

- Transplanting Method:

Select wet fields where the seedlings will not become dry, even in the case of a drought.

Plowing should be done between the last week of the second month and the first week of the third month.

Each paddy field is divided into ten parts: One part is for raising the seedlings and the other nine parts are for (transplanting) the seedlings. [When the seedlings have completely been picked (and transplanted into the other nine parts), also transplant them into the part where the seedlings were raised.]

First, plow the section where the seedlings will be grown according to the plowing method (mentioned previously), make the soil soft and

---

[11] F. H. King pointed out that vast extent of mountain lands in East Asia have long been taxed to their full capacity for fuel, timber, and herbage. Green manure and the ash of practically all the fuel used in the home find its way ultimately to the fields as fertilizer. However, but he missed Korea's unique process of thickly coating seeds directly with a urine–ash mixture, which produced almost as great a yield, with the added benefit of reducing the acidity of acid soils. Nowadays, the techniques are used for boosting the productivity of food crops. See Surendra K. Pradhan, Jarmo K. Holopainen, and Helvi Heinonen-Tanski, "Stored Human Urine Supplemented with Wood Ash as Fertilizer in Tomato (Solanum lycopersicum) Cultivation and Its Impacts on Fruit Yield and Quality," *Journal of Agriculture Food Chemistry*, Vol. 57, No. 16, pp. 7612–7617, 2009.

[12] In the "foot sowing" method, a farmer leaves a depressed hole in the soil, using his/her left heel, to throw a seed into the hole. Then, with right foot, dirt is thrown back into the hole to cover the seed.

leveled, and drain the water. Chop the soft ends of willow branches.[13] Spread them thickly all over the fields and then stamp them underfoot. Let the soil dry completely under the sun and (then) irrigate the field.

First, soak the seeds for three days. Then, put them in a *hoch'ŏn* [Its common name is *pinsŏm*.] to drain. After one day, plant the seeds in the soil and cover them (with soil) using a *p'allo*. [Its common name is *pŏnji*.]

When the seedlings have grown taller than the height of one's fist, they are able to be transplanted. First, plow the place where the seedlings will be transplanted. Then, spread the oak branches with leaves [Its common name is *chamkal*.] or cow or horse manure. When it is time to transplant the seedlings, plow again according to the method (mentioned previously) to make the soil loose and level, making it extremely soft. Plant four or five seedlings for each transplantation. Since they have not yet taken root, do not irrigate them deeply. [This method is convenient for weeding, in case of severe drought the crops will be lost, which is a matter of risk for the farm.]

- For the early-sowing rice seedbed:

Ashes and night soil should be mixed and spread over the early-sowing rice seedbed. If five *majigi*[14] of fields are used for several years as rice seedbeds, then spread three *sŏm*[15] of night soil mixed with ashes over them. If they are fields that are being used as rice seedbeds for the first time, then a mixture of four *sŏm* of night soil and ashes is appropriate. The night soil should be mixed in very smoothly. If the lumps in the night soil are not broken apart, then the seed grain will sit and float on the surface. [This method is practiced in the western area of Kyŏngsang Province.]

---

[13] The ends of weeping willows absorb soil acidity, which can help lower the pH. Seasoned farmers in Korea understand the basal application of fertilizer with willow which is a smart choice, as it contains a balance of the main nutrients nitrogen, phosphorus, and potassium. Vijay Singh Meena et al., *Potassium Solubilizing Microorganisms for Sustainable Agriculture*. Springer Nature Switzerland, 2018.

[14] The area is amount to the space needed for planting approximately 6 L of seeds.

[15] The volume *sŏm* is approximately 90 liters.

The hulls of sesame seeds are finely crushed and put in the stable, where they are stepped on by the livestock. Then, after winter passes, the hulls are gathered and mixed with cotton seeds and urine. This mixture fertilizes any kind of field. [This method is practiced by the people in the western area of Kyŏngsang Province. This same method for fertilizer is used even for late-sowing varieties of grain.]

- [The seedlings must be planted without being exposed to the sunlight] in the water of sandy rice seedbeds. Otherwise, they will not take root when the water soon dries out.

Generally, where the soil is not solid or the soil cannot be dried by the sunlight caused in rainfall, making the seedlings float on the water, drain the fields and push the seedlings down into the sand as needed, and then irrigate the fields after they take root.

- If the seedlings are still fragile even if the work of transplanting seedlings needs to be done quickly as the fields are about to dry out, if the rice seedbeds are filled with water, then the seedlings will naturally grow and come up above the water. However, they will be fragile and long, causing concern over whether they will disintegrate and rot during planting.

If the seedlings are not immediately transplanted when the appropriate time has passed, dots will form here and there like fly droppings. [Thus, they are commonly called "fly droppings."[16]] When the dots appear, dry grass should be spread over them, and then burnt and quenched immediately with water. Wait for the new shoots to appear (until they are) about the length of one *chon*[17] or when their length is judged appropriate. Then, if seedlings are transplanted, it will be as if the seedlings had been transplanted at the appropriate time. [One opinion says: "The rotting of the roots is prevented if a little water is poured over the flames, and they should be transplanted three days after."]

The *pǔnjong* method is for wet fields which face a water shortage, where the weeds flourish and cannot be easily removed. When the heads of grain are picked, tie the undamaged ones together, plow the weeds, and transplant (the seedlings) again. Then, the work of having to weed

---

[16] This refers to the rice blast fungus.
[17] About 2 cm.

every so often is drastically reduced. If this method is followed even if the fields have some water but there are not enough hands to weed, [then the grain will be plentiful, and this method is better than transplanting seedlings. Sometimes it is said, "There are not enough seedlings," but seasoned farmers who have experienced this many times, all say, "There will be plenty for planting."]

Take the leaves of the seedlings and soft willow branches and *chamgal* and chop them with a straw-cutter. They will float on top of the wet fields whether they are mixed with urine from the stables or from humans, stamped down on in the stables, or mixed with warm ashes and human urine. *Paektuongch'o* is also known as *chujŭgot* or *halmikkot*.[18] This is also good but highly poisonous and makes the seedlings rot if used in large quantities. The grass should be mixed following the above method and spread over the fields. [This practice is followed by the people of the eastern area of Kyŏngsang Province.]

Another method is mixing horse droppings, burnt leaves of seedlings, and human urine with ashes and gathering them in the ashery where they are covered with straw matting and grass to warm them up. This makes the seedlings float to the top when this is spread over the fields in the same manner as above. [Reeds are also quite good, but their flaw is that they grow too late to be used. However, as they grow day by day, transplanting seedlings can be done accordingly.]

- The fire weeding method [is not listed in CFT]

When the grain shoots sprout two or three leaves, first drain the water and spread dry grass evenly. If this is lit on fire and immediately quenched with water, the weeds will all die and only the grain will grow without having to weed, and (it will) double the crop yield. The people who plant five to six *sŏm* of seed grain, Nanjing, China, also use this method. However, this method is difficult to use if the dryness or humidity of the land cannot be adjusted as desired.

[One opinion states: "There will be no concern that the roots will be damaged if a little water is poured and then set alight."]

- Methods to plant mountainous rice:
- Though there are many varieties of rice, in general they are all alike. (However,) there is a special variety called *hando* [Its common name is *mebyŏ*.].

---

[18] Korean pasque flower.

Highlands and locations with sources of cold water are all appropriate (for this variety). However, if the soil is too dry, then this variety cannot grow.

Plow the soil in the first week of the second month, then plow again between the first and second week of the third month. Then, make ridges.

After finishing sowing by pressing the soil with heel resting on a pit, stamp down the ridges, making them hard.

When weeding, remove the soil around the sprouts to prevent them from being covered by soil.

If the soil is barren, mix (the seeds) with aged manure or ash and urine fertilizer and sow them. Alternatively, mix two parts *hando* seeds with two parts barnyard grass seeds and one part red beans and sow them. In general, this technique of mixing seeds and sowing them is (to prevent the loss of crops even in) years of flood or drought. As which of the nine grains will be appropriate for the following year's (weather conditions) differs, mixing seeds and sowing them help prevent a total loss.

- If an area where the grass is lush and trees are dense is to be newly cultivated and made into wet fields, then burn [them] and plow the soil.
- After three or four years, examine the soil quality and use manure.

If [the land] is marshes, swamps, and wasteland, then between the third and fourth months when the aquatic plants grow, use a *yunmok*[19] to kill the weeds, and wait until after the surface of the soil glistens to scatter seeds of the late-sowing variety.[20]

Also, tie two or three pieces of firewood and have it dragged by oxen to cover the seeds.[21] In the following year, a *chaenggi*[22] [Its common name is *Ttabi*.] may be used.

---

[19] The *yunmok* is thought to refer to a farming tool that is used to even out the soil (*namt'ae*).

[20] The edition held in the NLK has "長成" instead of "水草長成時," reading "水草成長時."

[21] *The edition held in the NLK has "業" for "柴," reading "又縛業木兩三箇."

[22] See Appendix B, No. XI; 木斫背 *mokchakpae, ssŏrae*.

In the third year, it is possible to plow with an ox. [If the foxtails do not grow, it will greatly reduce the work of weeding.] To make a *yunmok*, use strong and hardy wood four *ch'ŏk* long and cut its sides into five angles. Attach wooden rings at both ends of the wood, fastening them with a line. Seat a child on top of the saddle of an ox or horse, and with the rope tied to the wooden rings, tie to both sides of the *kyo*[23] [Its common name is *pukchi*.[24]] behind the saddle.[25] If the ox or horse moves, the five-angled *yunmok* revolves by itself, killing the weeds and breaking dirt clods. If the swamp is deep, and man and ox sink in it so that the soil cannot be stepped on, use a flail[26] [Its common name is *torikkae*.] to kill the weeds. Sowing the seeds is done the same as the above method.

References

F. H. King. *Farmers of Forty Centuries, or Permanent Agriculture in China, Korea and Japan*. Madison, 1911.

Kenneth Pomeranz. *The Great Divergence China, Europe, and the Making of the Modern World Economy*. Princeton: Princeton University Press, 2000.

---

[23] Stirrups.

[24] See Appendix B, No. X-2.

[25] See Appendix b, No. X-2; make from three or four pieces of split wood tied together, a tool used to level dirt which is also used for children to ride sleighs dragged by cows.

[26] See Appendix B, No. XII-1.

CHAPTER 13

Cultivating Proso/Foxtail Millet

Including Chŏmmulgok, Ch'ŏngnyang, *and* Sorghum

If the frost disappears in the third month [Early-sowing proso/foxtail millet should be sown in the first week of the third month. Late-sowing proso/foxtail millet should be sown between the second week of the third month and the first week of the fourth month.], select a good field. [Fields mixed with half fine sand and half black dirt are good. High and dry areas are appropriate for the nature of proso/foxtail millet, and low and wet places are not.] First, scatter red beans about the field. Then, plow.

Following the ridges, alternately step on and off with the left and right heels of one's feet. Sow a mix of wild sesame seeds with proso/foxtail millet. [One part wild sesame seeds, three parts proso/foxtail millet. By switching between left and right feet, the seeds will be covered with soil.[1]]

---

[1] This section is referring to the foot sowing method.

The edition held in the NLK does not have "附占勿谷粟. 青粱粟. 蜀黍."

When the seedlings grow, hoe and remove the weeds growing in between the seedlings. Where they are thick, cover up the roots with soil. Hoe three times, and do not stop hoeing just because there are no weeds.

After the seedlings have grown, if the weeds grow thickly between the ridges, yoke an ox with its mouth covered with a muzzle,[2] and have it plow slowly, preventing the plants from being damaged. [If there are no weeds between the ridges, cover the roots of the plants with soil.]

If the proso millet is half ripe, it should be cut immediately. For foxtail millet, it is possible to wait until it turns fully yellow to cut it. [When proso millet is ripe, it falls easily, and if it comes into contact with wind, then the harvest will be lost.]

If the fields are barren, use aged manure or urinated ash (for mixing) and sow the seeds. [For every two or three *toe* of millet, mix one *sŏm* of aged manure or urinated ash.]

- Proso/foxtail millet, as well, has a late-sowing quick-ripening variety [Its common name is *chŏmmulgok*.], similar to *ch'ŏngnyang* [Its common name is *saengdongchŏm*.].

Choose soil that is thick, old, and well-used for planting. [Places without trees and grass are best, old and well-used fields are second best, and fields where barley has been grown (and the roots remain) are worst.]

In the fifth month, remove the weeds, waiting till they are dry to burn them. When the ashes are not yet cool [If the ashes cool, then spiders make a web all over the field's surface, preventing the seeds from touching the soil.], scatter the proso/foxtail millet seeds. Then, dig up the earth with a *ch'ŏlch'ip'a* [Its common name is *susuŭm*.] and cover the seeds. This reduces the labor for hoeing and produces twice as much yield as normal.

[In general, regarding field cultivation methods, plowing in autumn (sow the seeds) grow in winter is best, and this is all the more so for proso/foxtail millet fields. If the stalks of intercropped proso/foxtail millet grow too thick due to rain, only the leaves will sprout, and the

---

[2] To stop the ox from eating the plants.

grain will not mature. Yoke an ox with its mouth covered with a muzzle, and plow in between two ridges, putting soil in between the joints of the proso/foxtail millet stalks. This will grow new roots and leaves that will grow long and mature into grain.]

- Sorghum [Its common name is *tangsŏ*.] is appropriate for low and wet areas, and inappropriate for high and dry areas. If sowed early in the second month, (even) without a second hoeing there will be a large harvest.[3]

---

[3]The edition in the NLK adds the following: The best days to plant beans are the *Chŏngsa, Ŭmyo, Shinmyo, Gimyo, Gimi, Byŏngcha, Muin, Imo,* and *Imin* days. The best day for planting sorghum is every three *myo* days of the third lunar month.

CHAPTER 14

Cultivating Barnyard Grass

Including Kangjik

It is possible to sow any time from the first week of the third month to the first week of the fourth month. The sowing method is the same as that of proso/foxtail millet. Alternatively, scattering the seeds is also fine. If the fields are barren, use aged manure and urinated ash. [Use aged manure and urinated ash in the following sections, as well.] Alternatively, first spread chopped weeds between the ridges prior to plowing and sowing. Hoeing (should be done) at least twice.

- Barnyard grass, as well, has a late-sowing quick-ripening variety. [Its common name is GangCHik Gang Barnyard Grass.] (This late-sowing quick-ripening variety) can be sown at the latest in the first week of the sixth month when relay cropping with barley/wheat.

Low and wetlands are appropriate for barnyard grass.
The soil (should be) plowed in the second week of the second month and well prepared with a *mokchak* [Its common name is *sohŭlla*.].
It is possible to sow any time from the first week of the third month to the first week of the fourth month. The sowing method is the same as that of proso/foxtail millet. Alternatively, scattering the seeds is also fine.
If the fields are barren, use aged manure and urinated ash. [Use aged manure and urinated ash in the following sections, as well.] Alternatively,

first spread chopped weeds between the ridges prior to plowing and sowing.

Hoeing (should be done) at least twice.

- Barnyard grass, as well, has a late-sowing quick-ripening variety. [Its common name is *kangchik*.] (This late-sowing quick-ripening variety) can be sown at the latest in the first week of the sixth month when relay cropping with barley or wheat.

CHAPTER 15

Cultivating Soybeans, Red Beans, and Mung Beans

Soybeans and red beans have early- and late-sowing varieties. [The early-sowing variety's common name is *Bomgali*. The late-sowing variety's common name is *Kŭlugali*. *Kŭlugali* refers to "plowing the roots of barley/wheat."][1]

The early-sowing variety can be sown from the second week of the third month to the second week of the fourth month.

When maintaining the fields, do not make the soil too soft. When sowing, do not put more than three or four seeds in each pit. [If there are many seeds, then they will grow densely, producing a small yield. Therefore, you should sow sparsely in fertile fields and densely in barren fields.]

If the fields are barren, use some aged manure and urinated ash, but not too much. Do not hoe more than twice. [When the flowers bloom, do not hoe, as it will make the flowers fall.]

When the leaves wither, harvest the beans. When the harvest ends, plow the fields and prepare for the following year. [If not plowed, then (the soil) becomes infertile.]

---

[1] It was not until 1888, led by the best scientists of all Europe, that it was conceded as demonstrated that leguminous plants acting as hosts for lower organisms living on their roots are responsible for the maintenance of soil nitrogen, drawing it directly from the air to which it is returned through the processes of decay. But in the fifteenth century, Korean seasoned farmers already used the practice of growing of legumes in rotation with barley, wheat, and foxtail millet.

- For the soybean *Kŭlugali* variety [immediately after barley/wheat is harvested, plow with the roots still in the soil], plowing, hoeing, and harvesting of the same as early-sowing varieties. However, in sowing, four or five seeds are to be put in each pit.
- The red bean *Kŭlugali* variety is the same as that of the soybean *Kŭlugali* variety. However, (for this variety you should) scatter the seeds on field where barley had been planted, then plow again. Hoe just once.
- One other method: In the case of small fields, when barley/wheat is ready to be harvested, make a small furrow in between their rows. Plant the soybeans in this furrow. Then, harvest the barley/wheat. Then using the dirt with the barley/wheat roots still in it, fill the furrow where the soybeans were planted.

The relay cropping of autumn barley in soybean fields and the relay cropping of foxtail millet in barley fields follow the same method as this.

- (The method of) plowing using an ox with its mouth covered with a muzzle is the same as for proso/foxtail millet fields. If weeds grow too much, then plow again.
- Mung beans can be sown in either barren fields or wastelands. Scatter them sparsely and hoe once.

[*Tongbu*[2] has the common name *tongbae*. It is planted in the fifth month in barren fields, hoed once, and harvested as soon as it ripens.]

---

[2] A specialty of Balhae (698–926), also known as Bohai, which was a multi-ethnic kingdom in Manchuria and the Korean peninsula. Most of CFT's techniques was an amalgamation of Balhae methods.

CHAPTER 16

Cultivating Barley and Wheat

Including Spring Barley.

As barley and wheat are planted between (this and the next year's) harvests, they are the most critical for farms.

Barren fields should be sown during White Dew,[1] acceptable fields should be sown during the Autumn Equinox, and fertile fields should be sown ten days after the Autumn Equinox.[2] (Sowing) too early is also bad. [There is an old saying: If sown early, then insects eat the plant while it grows joints.]

First, within the fifth and sixth months, plow the fields and expose them under the sun. Using a *mokchak* [Its common name is *sohŭlla*.] harrow them evenly. When it is time to sow, plow the fields again. After sowing is complete, use a *ch'ŏlch'ip'a* [Its common name is *susuŭm*.] or a *mokchakpae* [Its common name is *sohŭllabae*.] to deeply cover the seeds. [If sown early, then the roots grow deep and withstand cold, and if sown late, then the yield is small.]

In the third month of the following year, hoe the fields once. For fields where barley/wheat had been planted, refer to the previously mentioned method.

---

[1] "White Dew" refers to the 15th solar term beginning on September 7–8 and usually falling in the beginning of the eighth lunar month.

[2] "Autumn Equinox," or *ch'ubun*, refers to the 16th solar term, beginning on September 21 and usually falling at the middle of the eighth lunar month.

For fields where proso millet, beans, foxtail millet, and buckwheat had been planted, before the plant is harvested, use a large scythe with a long handle to cut the weeds before they turn yellow and stack them along the banks between the fields. After harvesting the grain, spread the weeds abundantly on top of the fields, burn them, then scatter the seeds, and plow the fields before the ashes disperse. For barren fields, spread twice the amount of weeds, and if the weeds could not be cut, use manure, or also, the method used for soybeans and red beans.

Alternatively, first sow mung beans or sesame. Then within the fifth or sixth month, wait until the plants are abundant for cutting and plowing.

Later, when sowing the seeds, plow and sow once more following the same methods as the ones previously mentioned.

- Between spring and summer, trim willow branches and spread them in the stable where the cows and horses are kept. Take them out every five or six days, stacking them to make manure. This is especially good for barley.
- Cut barley and wheat as they ripen. Immediately move them to a yard[3] and cover them with a straw mat to protect it from the rain. If they cannot (immediately) be moved to a yard, they must (at least) be moved to a high part of the field banks[4] and covered, then moved (to the yard) at night.

On a clear day, spread the barley and wheat thinly across the yard [If spread thickly, they will not dry well.] and thresh them as they dry. [(Milling)'s common name is *t'ajak*.]

There is nothing that busies a farmer more than barley and wheat. An old saying says: Gathering barley and wheat is like putting out a fire, if you slow down even a little, it results in disaster.

- For spring barley: Plowing can be done when the days become warmer in the second month and should be completed by the end of the second month. Sowing, hoeing, and harvesting methods are the same as that of autumn barley.

---

[3] This refers to a *madang* that one would find inside or in front of a traditional Korean house.

[4] This is referring to the high banks separating the fields from one another.

CHAPTER 17

Cultivating Sesame

Its common name is ch'amkkae. *It has the most oil among the* p'allŭng
Includes Perilla

Wasteland is appropriate (for sesame). [White soil is even better.]
In the fourth month after it rains [If it is not wet from the rain, it does not grow.], plow the soil and scatter the seeds. Use a *noemok* [Its common name is *koŭmp'a.*] to break up the dirt clods and cover the soil.

Hoe no more than twice.

Harvest (the sesame) as it ripens. Tie them into small bundles [Large bundles are hard to dry.] and make a pile by propping five or six bundles up against each other. When the fruit of the sesame opens, flip each bundle upside down and tap it lightly with a small stick. Once (the seeds) have been obtained, put (the fruits) in a pile as they were. Tap once every three days and (the seeds will completely fall out) after four or five times (of tapping).

For fertile fields: In the first week of the fourth month, in the case of fields where barley had been grown, immediately cut the barley, mix (the sesame seeds) with aged manure and urinated ash, and sparsely sow them on the root of barley.

Literally "eight edges/corners"; it is unclear precisely to what this is referring.

- One other method: Mix three parts white sesame with one part late-sowing red bean and sow the mixture. Or, mixing two parts mung bean with one part sesame is also fine. After plowing, make ridges, scatter the seed mixture evenly, and cover with soil.
- Sesamum indicum *Yuma* [Bencao[1] said "mayu" in the Tang dynasty Chinese people call chima. It is called *chamk'ae* in the countryside.]
- Perilla [Its common name is *tŭlkkae*.] should be sown on the roadside or field banks. Every pit is spaced one foot apart. If dense, then there will be no branches and a small yield.
- The method passed down among the people is transplanting the seeds between two furrows after the rains come about one ch'ŏk apart in fields where wheat or barley is plowed for double-cropping [transplant waiting for rain].

---

[1] The Tang herbology volume written by Su Gong associated with Changsun Wuji, which is China's most important traditional book on pharmaceuticals' guidelines and details of materia medica.

CHAPTER 18

Cultivating Buckwheat

Its common name is memil

It is good to get the right timing with buckwheat. [If the right time is missed and the frost comes, the harvest will be lost.] If the Autumn Equinox falls in the sixth month, then (the time to sow is) within three days before the Autumn Equinox. If the Autumn Equinox falls in the seventh month, then (the time to sow) is within three days after the Autumn Equinox.

Wastelands are appropriate (for planting buckwheat).

After plowing in the fifth month, wait for the grass to grow thick and plow again in the sixth month. Plow once again when sowing.

For one *mal* of seed, (mix) one *sŏm* of aged manure and urinated ash. [If lacking ashes, then drenching the seeds in water is fine.] Even if the fields are barren, if there is enough ash, then there can be a harvest.

If half of the grain is dark and half is light, then cut it. If turned upright, then all of it will darken.

In places with early frosts, plowing should be done early. There is no need to necessarily wait for the Autumn Equinox.

If the soil is fertile and dense due to forests, slash-and-burn farming will double the normal harvest.

- Seed Drenching Method: Prepare ash by burning cow and horse manure. Take urine from the stable and put it in a trough and soak (the seeds in the urine) for half a day. Then, take (the seeds) out (of the urine) and toss them into the ash so that they become completely covered (with ash).

The following is written in the edition of National Library of Korea.

CHAPTER 19

Cultivating Cotton

This is not written in (the 1429) CFT

Its nature suits fields that are dry mixed with sand. The fields are plowed completely and left alone in the second week of the second month. In the first week in the third month, the fields are plowed again and smoothed over with a *mokchak*. Plow once more when the seeds are sown.

It is sometimes planted on the third day of the third month, which frequently doubles its crop yield. It is also sometimes planted during Grain Rain[1] or Summer Commences.[2] Usually if planted early, it will be plentiful even if frost falls.

Mix the cotton seeds gently with cow manure, wait until their white color cannot be seen, and then cover them in a urine and ash mixture, and cover them again with dried ashes until they are the size of hazelnuts.

After the ridges are made, sharpen the bottom ends of the *noemok* and puncture holes along the top of the ridges. Make the holes wide enough that there will be no problems in planting the seeds.

---

[1] "Grain Rain," or *Kok-u*, refers to the 6th solar term, beginning on April 20 and usually falling at the middle of the third lunar month.

[2] "Summer Commences," or *Ip'ha*, refers to the 7th solar term, beginning on May 6 and usually falling at the beginning of the fourth lunar month.

Put urine and cow and horse manure in the holes and sow the seeds. Then cover (the holes) with a *milgae*. Nothing bad will come out of frequent weeing, and if weeds grow in between the ridges, then yoke an ox and cover its mouth with a mesh bag and plow so as not to damage the plants.

- People in the country make a intercropping with sesame or green beans, but they do not know the damages for the harvest of cotton. Who know the harmful effect never make an intercropping, only focus on the cotton. [The people of *Okch'ŏn* and *Yangsan* follow this method.]
- For barren fields in mountain valleys or plains, dig a wide pit about the width of seat cushion and the depth of the knees after the ice has melted. When the time comes to plant cotton seeds, fill it with urine and cow or horse manure, and cover it with fresh dirt. Cover the cotton seeds in cow urine or clumped ashes to the size of chestnuts and plant five or six in the pit. When they grow to seven to eight *ch'on* or the shoots sprout, the plants will grow and the crop yield will double. If this is done again on the surface of the pit the following year, it will become a fertile field after three years. [This is the practical method by *Yunchowon*.[3] There is no farmland that does not his way.]

---

[3] Who is the most famous agriculturalist in the sixteenth-century Chosŏn.

Appendix A: Original Text of CFT and Photos CFT 1 Kyujanggak Royal Library the 1581 Edition and CFT 2 the National Library of Korea 1655 Edition

農事直說 序文
○命摠制鄭招等撰農事直說
其序曰 農者, 天下國家之大本也. 自古聖王莫不以是爲務焉. 帝舜之命九官十二牧也,首曰:食哉惟時, 誠以粢盛之奉, 生養之資, 捨是無以爲也.
恭惟太宗恭定大王嘗命儒臣, 掇取古農書, 切用之語, 附註鄕言, 刊板頒行, 敎民力本.
及我主上殿下, 繼明圖治, 尤留意於民事,
以五方風土不同, 樹藝之法, 各有其宜, 不可盡同古書, 乃命諸道監司逮訪州縣老農, 因地已試之驗具聞.
又命臣招就加詮, 次臣與宗簿小尹臣卞孝文, 披閱參考, 祛其重複. 取其切要, 撰成一編, 目曰農事直說.
農事之外, 不雜他說, 務爲簡直, 使山野之民, 曉然易知.
旣進下鑄字所, 印若干本, 將以頒諸中外, 導民厚生, 以至於家給人民也.
臣竊觀周詩, 周家以農事爲國, 歷八百餘年之久.
今我殿下惠養斯民, 爲國長慮, 豈不與后稷成王同一規範乎?
是書雖小, 其爲利益, 可勝言哉.

農事直說 本文

備穀種
收九穀種, 取堅實不雜不浥者.【浥, 鬱浥也. 種不實, 則明年穀穗亦不實, 所謂受病於胎也. 種雜, 則早晚不等; 種浥, 則不生, 雖生亦不實】簸揚去

秕, 後沉水去浮者, 漉出曬乾. 以十分無濕氣爲度. 堅藏蒿篅之類.【蒿篅, 鄕名空石. 小有濕氣[1] 多致鬱浥.】
○欲知來歲所宜, 以九穀種各一升各盛布裹, 埋於土宇中.【勿令人坐臥其上.】 後五十日, 發取量之, 息冣多者,[2] 其歲所宜也. 土氣隨地異宜, 宜令各村[3] 里試之[4].
○冬月, 以瓮或[5] 槽埋地中, 要令不凍. 至臘月, 多收雪汁盛貯, 苫薦【鄕名飛介】厚盖.【古書曰: 雪五穀之精.】 至種時, 漬種其中, 漉出[6] 曬乾, 如此二度.[7] 或用木槽, 盛牛馬廐池尿, 漬種其中, 漉出曬乾,[8] 亦須三度.
○ 耕地

耕地宜徐. 徐則土軟, 牛不疲困. 春夏耕宜淺, 秋耕宜深.
春耕, 則隨耕隨治, 秋耕, 則待土色乾白, 乃治.
○ 旱田, 初耕後, 布草燒之, 又耕, 則其田自美.
○ 薄田, 耕, 菉豆待其茂盛, 掩耕, 則不莠不虫, 變堉爲良.[9]
○ 荒地,[10] 七八月間耕之掩草, 明年氷釋, 又耕後, 下種. 大抵荒地開墾, 初耕宜深, 再耕宜淺, [初深後淺, 則生地不起, 令土軟熟].

○ 荒地辨試之法.
劚土一尺深, 嘗其味.
甛者爲上, 不甛不醶者次之, 醶者爲下.
○ 濕田, 不宜種穀處, 經霜後, 刈草刓之, 厚布田中, 種小麥則麥極好, 而翌年變爲乾田, 至種, 木花亦宜. [慶尙左道人 行之]

---

[1] The edition held in the NLK omits 小 in "小有濕氣."
[2] The edition held in the NLK has 不 in front of 息冣多者 as 冣.
[3] The edition held in the NLK omits 村 in "宜令各里試之."
[4] The edition held in the NLK has the following characters attached: 俗方 或冬至 埋置 立春日 出之.
[5] The edition held in the Changsŏgak Archives omits 或 in "以瓮槽埋地中."
[6] The edition held in the Changsŏgak Archives omits "漉出" in 漬種其中, 曬乾.
[7] The edition held in the NLK has "如此三度" rather than "如此二度."
[8] The edition held in the NLK says "漬種其中, 漉出(日+丣)乾" here.
[9] The edition held by the NLK adds the following: 凢美田之法 菉豆爲上, 小豆胡麻(眞荏)次之, 五六月中穊種, 七八月犁掩殺之, 爲春穀田, 則畝收十石.
[10] The edition held in the NLK has "荒田" instead of "荒地."

○ 種麻
正月氷解, 擇良田. 田多, 則歲易. 【歲易, 則皮薄節闊[11]】 耕之縱三橫三, 布牛馬糞, 二月上旬, 更耕之. 【中旬爲中時, 下旬爲下時. 至於北土, 寒氣晚解, 要當隨時適宜. 九穀做此.】
以木斫【鄕名斫訖羅】及鐵齒擺【鄕名手愁音】, 熟治使平, 後足踏均密. 撒種, 又須均須密. 【足踏與撒種, 不均不密, 則麻或龘或枝, 不中於用.】 曳撈覆種. 【撈, 鄕名曳介. 編多枝木爲之, 松枝爲上.】 其上, 又布牛馬糞. 麻長三寸許, 有雜草, 則鋤之. 【不過一鋤. 又有晚種者, 夏至前後十日內, 皆可種也.】[12]

○ 種稻 附旱稻[13]
稻種有早有晚. 耕種法有水耕【鄕名: 水沙彌】有乾耕【鄕名: 乾沙彌】, 又有揷種【鄕名: 苗種】. 除草之法, 則[14] 大抵皆同.
○早稻:
秋收後, 擇連水源肥膏水田, 【凡水田, 上可以引水, 下可以決去. 旱則灌之, 雨則洩之者, 爲上. 洿下渟水處, 次之, 然久雨泥渾, 則苗腐. 高處須雨而耕者, 斯爲下矣.[15]】 耕之.
冬月入糞. 【正月氷解, 耕之入糞. 或入新土亦得.】 二月上旬又耕之. 以木斫【鄕名: 所訖羅】縱橫摩平, 復以鐵齒擺【鄕名: 手愁音】打破土塊令熟.
先以稻種漬水, 經三日, 漉出, 納蒿篅中【鄕名: 空石】, 置溫處, 頻頻開視, 勿致鬱浥. 芽長二分, 均撒水田中, 以板撈【鄕名: 翻地[16]】或把撈【鄕名: 推介】覆種.[17] 灌水驅鳥.【以苗生爲限】

---

[11]The edition in the NLK has "茚" instead of "節" in "則皮薄茚闊."

[12]The following are added in the edition held in the NLK: The *Sinsa, Musin, Sinhae, Kihae, Gapsin, and Gyŏngsin* days are good for planting hemp, while every five, eleven, eight, six days in the four seasons are to be avoided. The best day to plant is on the three *myo* days of the first lunar month.

[13]The following are added in the edition held in the NLK 附 晚稻 稻忌 寅 卯 辰□ 宜 戊 己 四月□ 季朔 十八□ 季□也.

[14]The edition held in the NLK omits "則."

[15]. The edition held in the NLK omits "者" from "雨則洩之爲上." and has "傳" instead of "渟" in "洿下渟水處次之," and the edition held in the Jangseogak Archives omits "矣" from "斯爲下矣."

[16]The edition held in the Jangseogak Archives has "畨+月" for "飜" in "鄕名飜地."

[17]*The edition held in the Jangseogak Archives has "畨+月" for "飜" in "鄕名飜地."

苗生二葉, 則去水, 以手耘.【苗弱, 不可用鋤.[18] 然水渴土强, 則當用鋤.】 去苗間細草, 訖又灌水【每去水而耘, 耘訖灌之. 苗弱時宜淺, 苗强時宜深】 如川水連通, 雖旱不渴處, 則每耘訖決去水, 曝根二日, 後還灌水【耐風與旱】

苗長半尺許, 又耘以鋤.【苗强, 可以用鋤】 耘時, 以手接軟苗間土面. 耘至三四度,【禾穀成長,[19] 唯賴鋤功 且旱稻性速, 不可小緩】 將熟去水【有水, 則熟遲】 旱稻善零, 隨熟隨刈.

○晚稻水耕:

正月氷解耕之. 入糞入土, 與旱稻法同.【今年入土, 則明年入糞[20] 或入雜草, 互爲之.】 其地或泥濘或虛浮或水冷, 則專入新土或莎土; 瘠薄, 則布牛馬糞及連枝杻葉【鄕名: 加乙草】, 人糞蠶沙亦佳.【但多得爲難】

三月上旬至芒種節, 又耕之.【大抵節[21] 晚耕種者, 不實.】

漬種, 下種, 覆種, 灌水, 耘法, 皆與旱稻法同.【六月望前三度耘者, 爲上. 六月內三度耘者, 次之. 不及此者爲下.】

○ (乾耕):

春旱不可水耕, 宜乾耕.【唯種晚稻】

其法, 耕訖, 以檑木【鄕名: 古音波】打破土塊, 又以木斫【鄕名 所訖羅】 縱橫摩平, 熟治後, 以稻種一斗和熟糞或尿灰一石爲度【作尿灰法: 牛廐外, 作池貯尿, 以穀稭及糠秕之類, 燒爲灰, 用所貯池尿拌均.】, 足種.

驅鳥.【以苗生爲限】苗未成長,[22] 不可灌水. 雜草生, 則雖旱苗槀, 不可停鋤.【古語曰[23]「鋤頭自有百本禾.」 老農亦曰: 「苗知人功.」】

○苗種法: 擇水田雖遇旱不乾處. 二月下旬至三月上旬可耕. 每水田十分, 以一分養苗, 餘九分以擬栽苗.【拔苗訖, 幷栽養苗處.】 先耕養苗處如法, 熟治, 去水, 剉柳枝軟梢厚布, 訖足踏之. 曝土令乾, 後灌水. 先漬稻種三日, 漉入[24] 蒿篅【鄕名: 空石】 經一日下種, 後以板撈【鄕名: 翻地[25]】覆種. 苗長一握以上, 可移栽之. 先耕苗種處, 布杻葉【鄕名: 加乙

---

[18]The edition held in the NLK adds "末" in "苗弱, 不可用末鋤."

[19]The edition held in the NLK has "長成" for "禾穀長成."

[20]The edition held in the Jangseogak Archives omits "則" from "明年入糞."

[21]The edition held in the Jangseogak Archives has "莭" instead of "節" in "大抵節晚耕種者."

[22]The edition held in the NLK has "長成" for "苗未長成, 不可灌水."

[23]The edition held in the NLK has "云" instead of "曰" in "古語云."

[24]The edition held in the NLK has "出" instead of "入" in "漉入蒿篅," reading "漉出入蒿篅."

[25]In both editions held in Jangseogak Archives and the NLK, "飜" in "鄕名飜地" is written as "番+月."

草】或牛馬糞. 臨移栽時, 又耕之如法, 熟治, 令土極軟. 每一科栽不過四五苗.[26] 根未着土, 灌水不可令深.【此法, 便於除草, 萬一大旱,[27] 則失手, 農家之危事也.[28]】

○ 早稻秧基
以灰和人糞, 布秧基, 而假如五斗落, 多年秧基, 則和糞灰三石. 若初作秧基, 則和糞灰四石適中. 和糞時, 極細調均. 若糞塊未破, 穀着其上, 反致浮釀. [慶尙左西道行之]
胡麻殼剉之, 牛馬廐踐踏, 積置經冬者, 木綿子和廐尿者, 亦可.
[右道人行之 莭早無草 則可好而至於晩稻亦爲之]
○ 沙沓秧基, 因水下種, 不然暫乾秧, 不着根. [不待曝土而下種]
凡地品不强, 或因雨水, 不得如法, 曝土處有秧種浮釀之狀, 則去水, 如根未着土, 以沙量宜厭之, 根着後貯水.
○ 移秧處. 水若乾涸. 急於移栽. 而苗弱. 若儲水秧基. 則秧苗自然 出水長成. 然弱而長. 移種時. 不無折傷之患矣.
○ 苗種, 或不卽移秧(挿), 有過時蠅點ською, [俗所謂蠅尿]. 厚布乾草於苗上, 焚之後卽灌水, 待其葉間新芽抽出寸許, 或量宜長短秧種, 則與趂時 挿秧者無異, 上同. [一說 小灌水焚之 無傷根 三日後種之].
反種法: 水田無水, 雜草荒蕪, 未易除(去)却處, 待水拔取禾苗, 不至損傷者束之, 反耕更種, 一如苗種法, 則鋤功甚省. 雖有水處, 人力不足, 難於除草, 則亦行此法. 禾甚盛, 勝於苗種, 或云禾不足, 而老農屢經之, 人皆曰足以種矣.
○ 秧草, 軟柳枝及眞櫟, ㅈ·ㅁ갈 以負斫刀, 似挾刀 下鐵以木爲柄
打斷, 用廐下水, 或人尿沾濕, 或牛馬廐踐踏, 和溫灰及人尿積置, 以苦草蓋之善蒸, 白頭翁草, 亦可而甚毒, 多布傷秧, 須雜以芳草, 俗小兒作髮細草之類也 如上法蒸而用之. 慶尙左道人 行之 又方馬糞燒灰, 有火秧草, 交合人尿, 雜以火灰積之, 灰基以苦草盖之, 煖鬱速蒸, 上同. ○ 蘆草甚好, 而可欠晚, 然日日苗長, 可以計月, 移秧.
○ 火耨法 [直說不錄]
禾苗, 至兩三葉, 則先放水, 乾草量宜均布, 以火焚之, 卽爲灌水, 則雜草盡死. 苗長自茁, 雖不鋤耨, 所收倍多, 中國南京一人, 至種五六石之多者, 用此法也. 然非燥濕任意之處, 則決難行之, 上同.
[一說, 小灌水焚之, 無傷根之患, 過時草盛, 難鋤之畓, 以木斫 所訖羅 駕牛摩治, 如初種時, 旋卽鋤之, 則易耨而苗盛.]

[26] The edition held in the NLK has "三四" for "四五," reading "每一科栽不過三四苗."

[27] *The edition in the Jangseogak Archives has "旱" in "萬一大旱," reading "萬一大旱." The edition in the NLK omits "之" in "農家之危事也," reading "農家危事也."

[28] The edition in the NLK omits "之" in "農家之危事也," reading "農家危事也."

種山稻法
○稻種甚多. 大抵皆同, 別有一種, 曰旱稻【鄕名: 山稻[29]】.
徧宜於高地及水冷處, 然土大燥則不成. 二月上旬耕之. 三月上旬至中旬, 又耕之, 作畝足種. 訖踏畝背令堅. 耘時, 去苗間土勿擁. 地若瘠薄, 和熟糞或尿灰, 種之. 或旱稻二分,[30] 稷二分, 小豆一分, 相和而種.【大抵雜種[31] 之術, 以歲有水旱. 九穀隨歲異宜, 故交種, 則不至全失.】
○ 若新墾草木茂密處, 爲水田者, 火而耕之. 三四年後, 審其土性, 用糞.
○ 若沮澤潤濕荒地, 則三四月間, 水草成長時,[32] 用輪木殺草, 待土面融熟後, 下晚稻種. 又縛柴[33] 木兩三箇, 曳之以牛, 覆其種. 至明年, 可用耒 [鄕名地寶].
三年, 則可用牛耕 [粮莠不生, 大省鋤功].
其輪木之制, 用堅强[34] 木, 長可四尺, 爲五銳隅, 兩頭貫木環, 以繩繫環.
令兒童騎粧鞍牛或馬, 以繫環繩, 結鞍後橋 [鄕名北枝] 兩旁. 牛馬行, 則其輪木五銳隅, 自回轉, 殺草破塊. 若沮甚, 人牛陷沒, 不可入蹈之地, 用栲栳 [鄕名都里鞭] 殺草. 下種一如前法.
○種黍, 粟【附占勿谷粟, 靑梁粟, 蜀黍】:
三月霜氣頓無,【早黍, 早粟, 三月上旬, 晚黍, 晚粟, 三月中旬至四月上旬, 可種.】擇良田,【細沙, 黑土相半者爲良. 黍, 粟, 性宜高燥, 不宜下濕.[35]】
先用小豆稀疎播撒, 後耕之. 遂畝左右足踵交踏,[36] 以水荏子與黍或粟, 相和【水荏子一分, 黍或粟三分.】下種.【左右足交運, 已成覆土矣.】
及苗長, 間生雜草與科密處, 鋤而去之, 以土壅根. 鋤至三度, 勿以無草停鋤.

[29]One of the most important resources needed for farming is cultivars of crops that are suited to grow in climates change. Many upland areas do not have as easy access to usable water leading to breeds becoming naturally more resistant to drought-like conditions. Using these methods is important to growing productive rice.

[30]The edition in the NLK has "三" instead of "二," reading "或旱稻三分."

[31]If this term translate into crossbreed or hybridization is wrong translation. In crops plant this term should translate "companion cropping mixing seeds and sowing." This is the best technology of Korean agriculture can help grow bountiful crops with any climate shock. Korean seasoned farmers have suiliciently appreciated the fact that companion cropping and intercropping have the potential to produce up crop yield while also allowing for a reduction in off-farm inputs.

[32]*The edition held in the NLK has "長成" instead of "水草長成時," reading "水草成長時."

[33]*The edition held in the NLK has "業" for "柴," reading "又縛業木迺三箇."

[34]*The edition held in the NLK has "剛" for "强," reading "用堅剛木."

[35]The edition held in the NLK adds "地" at the end, reading "不宜下濕地."

[36]The edition held in the NLK has "種" for "踵," reading "左右足種交踏."

待禾成長, 兩畝間雜草茂盛, 用一牛網其口, 徐驅耕之, 勿致損禾.【畝間無穢, 土壅禾根.】
黍半熟卽刈, 粟待十分黃熟可刈.【黍熟易零, 遇風卽失收.】
田若塉薄, 用熟糞或尿灰, 種之.【每黍, 粟二三升, 和熟糞或尿灰一石爲度.】
○ 粟又有晚種早熟, 如靑梁【鄕名生動粘】之類者.【鄕名占勿谷】 擇土厚久陳地, 種之.【芟除林木爲上,[37] 久陳田次之, 麥根爲下.】
五月伐草, 待乾火之. 灰未冷時,【灰冷卽蜘蛛遍網地面, 種不至地.】
撒擲粟種, 以鐵齒擺【鄕名手愁音[38]】, 起土覆種粟, 鋤草省力, 所出倍常.【大抵治田之法, 秋耕過冬爲上, 粟田尤甚.】
○ 間種之粟, 或因雨澤, 莖節過爲茂盛穗而不實, 網牛口耕, 兩畝間掩土於莖節, 則更生, 新根穗長而實.
○ 蜀黍【鄕名唐黍】, 宜下濕, 不宜高燥. 二月早種, 鋤不至再而收多.
○種稷【附姜稷】:
稷性宜下濕之地. 二月中旬耕地, 以木斫【所訖羅[39]】熟治. 自三月上旬至四月上旬, 皆可種. 種法與種黍粟同, 或撒擲種亦得. 田若塉薄, 用糞灰,【熟糞與尿灰也. 下倣此.】 或先布雜草於畝間, 後耕種. 鋤至二度.
○稷亦有晚種早熟者.【鄕名姜稷】 兩麥底六月上旬可種.
○種大豆○小豆○菉豆[40]:
大豆, 小豆, 種, 皆有早有晚.【早種鄕名春耕, 晚種鄕名根耕. 根耕者, 耕兩麥根也.】
早種, 三月中旬至四月中旬可種也. 治田不可過熟. 下種每科不過三四箇.【下種多, 則茂密少實. 然肥田種欲稀, 薄田種欲稠.】
田若塉薄, 用糞灰, 宜小不宜多. 鋤不過再.【吐花時不可鋤, 令花落.】
葉盡收之. 收訖耕之, 以擬明年.【不耕卽無澤.】
○大豆根耕.【刈兩麥, 旋耕其根也.】 耕耘及收皆與早種同. 但下種每科四五箇.
○小豆根耕, 與大豆根耕同. 但撒種於麥根, 訖覆耕之. 一鋤而止.
○又一法, 田小者, 兩麥未穗時, 淺耕兩畝間, 種以大豆. 收兩麥, 訖又耕麥根, 以覆豆根. 大豆田間種秋麥, 麥田間種粟, 皆同此法.
○用網口牛, 耕兩畝間, 與黍粟田同. 雜草還茂, 則再耕之.

---

[37]The edition in the Jangseogak Archives has "禾" for "木," reading 芟除林禾爲上.

[38]*The edition in the NLK omits "鄕名手愁音."

[39]The edition in the NLK omits known locally as sohŭlla (所訖羅).

[40]*The edition in the NLK has the following: Beans dislike the days of *Myoo (Muo), Byŏngcha, Gapŭl*, the appropriate days is *Gapcha, Im. Red beans as same.*

○菉豆, 薄田荒地, 皆可種也. 稀種. 一鋤.⁴¹ 【撤種 (亦)得】
○豌豆 【鄉名 同輩.】 五月間種薄田 一鋤 隨熟摘之

種大小麥 【附春麰】:
大小麥, 新舊間接食, 農家寂急.⁴² 薄田白露節,⁴³ 中田秋分時, 美田後十日可種. 大早又不可, 【古語曰: 早種, 則蟲而有節.】 先於五六月間, 耕之曝陽, 用木斫【鄉名所訖羅⁴⁴】摩平. 下種時又耕之. 下種訖以鐵齒擺 【鄉名: 手愁音】或木斫背【鄉名: 所訖羅背⁴⁵】覆種宜厚. 【早種, 則根深耐寒; 晚種, 則穗小.】
明年三月間, 一鋤之. 麥根田, 則依上法. 黍, 豆, 粟, 木麥根田, 則預於收穀前, 用長柄大鎌. 及草未黃時刈之, 積在田畔, 收穀訖以其草厚布田上, 火焚, 擲種, 及灰未散耕之. 薄田倍加布草, 如未及刈草, 用糞, 又如大小豆法.
或於其田, 先種菉豆或胡麻, 五六月間掩耕, 待草爛後下種時, 又耕種之, 如前法.
○春夏間刴細柳枝, 布牛馬廄, 每五六日取出, 積之爲糞. 甚宜於麥.
○大小麥隨熟隨刈, 卽輸⁴⁶ 於場. 用苫盖覆, 以防雨作. 若不及輸場, 亦須輸運於田畔高處盖覆, 乘夜輸入, 遇晴以麥薄布場上, 【厚則難乾.】 隨乾隨輾【輾, 鄉名: 打作.】
農家所忙, 無過於麥. 古語曰: 「取麥如救火」, 若小遲慢, 終爲災傷.
○春麰: 二月間陽氣溫和日可耕, 盡二月止. 種法, 耘法,⁴⁷ 收法與秋麥同. [麥芒 八月中 不出者 白蘘荷根莖取汁 注目中即出]
○ 七月, 刈白蘘軟枝, 櫟木갈枝葉, 杻枝, 굴쌀이 以負斫刀絶斷, 作坎積置, 廄池水注濕, 或牛馬廄踐踏, 待蒸糞田, 則至種雜穀 無不茂盛, 而尤宜兩麥, 上同. 秋間茄子盡摘後, 收乾莖葉藏之, 明年刴入, 秧基極好. ○ 櫟枝葉 至秋刈取 經冬 踏於牛馬廄 [嶺南左道人行之]
○ 兩麥收時, 農務正急焉, 刈麥作束, 田畔高處, 以長木如土宇狀交搆, 將麥束積之, 穗向內, 根向外, 鱗次密積, 作穴一面, 則風不拐, 而雨不漏, 農歇後打入, 但場畔, 則雖或如右積之, 必生飛蛾忌之.

---

⁴¹*The edition in the NLK has the following: The best days to plant beans are the *Gapcha, Ŭlchuk, Imsin, Byŏngcha, Muin, Imo, and Imin* days. The best day for planting beans is three myo days of the sixth lunar month.

⁴²The edition in the Library of Korea has "最" for "寂."

⁴³The edition in the Jangseogak Archives has "茆" for "節," reading "薄田白露茆."

⁴⁴The edition in the NLK omits "鄉名所訖羅."

⁴⁵The edition in the NLK omits "鄉名手愁音," "鄉名所訖羅背."

⁴⁶The edition in the NLK has "收" for "輸," reading "卽收於場."

⁴⁷The edition in the Jangseogak Archives omits "耘法" from "種法. 收法, 與秋麥同."

種胡麻【鄉名眞荏子. 八稜者多油.[48]】【附油麻.】: 性宜荒地.【白壤尤良.】
四月間雨後,【不因雨則不生.】耕地撒種. 用檑木【鄉名: 古音波】, 破塊覆土. 鋤不過再. 隨熟刈之. 作束欲小.【束大難乾.】五六束相倚爲叢. 候口開, 逐束倒竪, 以小杖輕打, 取了還叢之. 三日一打, 四五遍乃盡. 若熟田則四月上旬, 麥根田則趂刈麥後, 和糞灰稀種.
○又一法: 以白胡麻三分. 晚小豆一分相和種之. 或以菉豆二分. 胡麻一分相和亦得.
耕訖, 作畝, 以所和種, 均撒, 覆土.
○油麻,【本草白油麻, 唐人稱芝麻, 俗所爲眞荏子.】水蘇子.【俗稱水荏子】
○水蘇子,【俗稱水荏子】路邊或田畔宜種. 每科相去一尺【密則無枝少實.】
○俗方 四月上旬 苗種 兩麥根耕時 移種 兩畝間相去尺餘【乘雨揷之】

種蕎麥【鄉名木麥】: 蕎麥趂時爲良.【失時遇霜不收.】
立秋在六月, 則節前三日內, 立秋在七月, 則節後三日內, 乃其時也.
宜荒地. 五月耕之. 得草爛, 六月又耕. 下種時, 又耕之.
種子一斗, 糞灰一石爲度.【灰小, 則漬種亦可.】田雖堉薄, 多糞灰, 則可收.
其實半黑半白, 刈之。倒竪, 則皆黑。 其早霜處, 宜早耕, 不必待立秋前後也.
若山林肥厚之地, 火耕撒種, 所收倍常.
○漬種法: 燒牛馬糞爲灰, 以廁池尿盛貯木槽中, 漬蕎麥種半日, 漉出. 投灰中, 令灰粘着種子.

種木花法【直說不錄】
性宜雜沙燥田, 二月中旬翻耕, 三月上旬又耕之, 以木斫熟治, 下種時更耕.【或三月三日下種, 所收倍多, 或穀雨下種, 或立夏前下種, 蓋早耕, 則雖有霜, 結裹必多.】綿種先, 以牛糞挼磨, 以白色盡沒爲度, 多粘尿灰, 轉着乾灰, 箇大如榛, 成畝後, 檑木尖其下端, 打穴畝上,【隨畝狹作穴多小】以尿灰或牛馬糞先行布穴【作穴頗廣下種無礙.】後撒種, 以推介掩土, 鋤不厭多, 待其長成, 畝間草茂, 用一牛網口, 徐耕勿致損傷.
○ 世之糞田者, 未耕前, 撒糞田中, 其功不專於根, 莫如此法之爲善也.
○ 俗人, 有間種眞荏靑太 而不知損害木花 專業摘花者 絶不間種【沃川陽山人行之.】

[48]The edition in the NLK adds "油黑者曰勝."

○ 山谷或平原荒田, 解氷後, 掘坎沒脛, 廣如方席, 種木綿臨時, 尿灰與牛馬糞塡炕, 又加新土, 以綿種, 轉着牛尿及熟灰, 如栗子大, 一坑種五六箇, 待長成約七八寸, 去其上枝, 則枝茂棄蕃, 所摘倍多, 明年坑傍又如是, 則三年後, 終便爲饒田, 無墾耕之功而最利焉.

農事直說 字音義
浥 裏同潤也
穗 音遂與穟同
簸 音橎揚去穮也
秕 音比穀皮也
漉 音鹿瀝也
曬 音灑日乾也
篅 音遄草器盛穀者
苫 失廉切編草具
屎 徒小切腹中水也
莠 音誘 禾穗而不成者
堉 音籍薄也
𪒟 陟玉切也
甜 徒兼舌甘也
擺 補買切 撒 音散散也
捞 音勞
挿 楚洽切刺入
秧 音決
洩 音曳漏洩
洿 音烏獨水不流
耐 奴代切忍也
挼 奴禾切兩手相切摩也
濘 音佞泥濘
杼 音序橡也亦謂櫟
㯒 力埵切
秸 乃黠切禾稾
穅 音康穀皮
拌 音伴
刐 蠡臥切破也
銳 以芮切利也
栲 音考
栳 音老
菉 直綠切
梁 音梁

䴴 音牟大麥也
輾 哲善切水輾
堅 音樹立也
蕎 音喬

APPENDIX A: ORIGINAL TEXT OF CFT AND PHOTOS ...   125

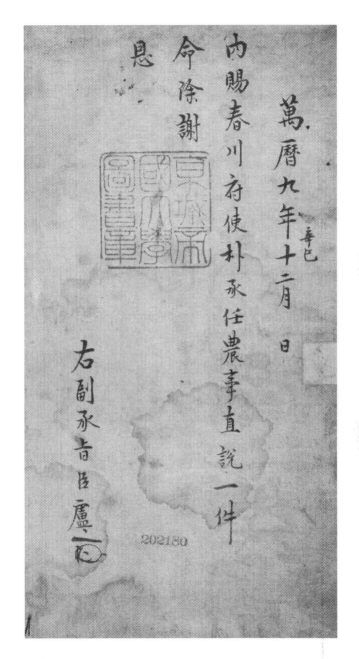

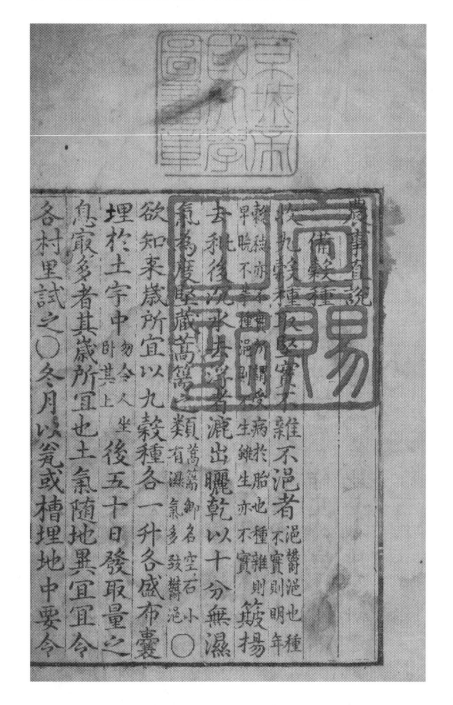

不凍至臘月多收雪汁盛貯苫薦卿名厚蓋

古書曰雪五穀之精至種時漬種其中溉出曬乾如此

二度或用木槽盛牛馬厩池尿漬種其中溉

出曬乾亦湏三度

耕地

耕地宜徐徐則土軟牛不疲困春夏耕宜淺

秋耕宜深春耕則隨耕治秋耕則待土色

乾白乃治〇旱田初耕後布草燒之又耕則

其田自美〇薄田耕菉豆待其茂盛掩耕則

不糞不蚕變塉為良〇荒地七八月間耕之

掩草明年冰釋又耕後下種大抵荒地開墾
初耕宜深再耕宜淺﹝初深後淺則生地不起令土軟熟﹞○荒
地辨試之法斸土一尺深嘗其味甜者為上
不甜不鹹者次之鹹者為下
種麻
正月冰解擇良田田多則歲易﹝歲易剛皮薄節闊﹞耕
之縱三橫三布牛馬糞二月上旬更耕之﹝旬
為中時下旬為下時至於北土寒以此斸﹞以木斫﹝各鄉名手﹞熟治使平後足踏均
所荒及鐵齒擺﹝愁音﹞
宓撒種又須均須宓則足踏與撒種不均不宓則麻或飽或瘦不中

APPENDIX A: ORIGINAL TEXT OF CFT AND PHOTOS ... 129

用曳撈覆種木鄉名曳介編多枝其上又布牛馬糞麻長三寸許有雜草則鋤之鋤又有

種稻附早稻
晚種者夏至前後十日內皆可種也

稻種有早有晚耕種法有水耕沙鄉名水有乾彌又有挿種苗鄉名除草之法則大抵耕沙鄉名乾彌

皆同〇早稻秋收後擇連水源肥膏水田犯田上可以引水下可以決去之旱則灌之雨則洩之者為上淊下淖水濕次次之然久雨渾則耕之冬月入糞正月入糞解

土或兩則耕黃齒為下矣耕之雨者斯為高燥須入新得二月上旬又耕之以木斫訖鄉名羅所縱

橫摩平復以鐵齒擺鄉名手愁音打破土塊令熟
先以稻種漬水經三日漉出納蒿篅中空石鄉名
置溫處頻頻開視勿致鬱浥芽長二分均撒
水田中以板撈鄉名地或把撈鄉名介覆種灌水
驅鳥以齒生苗不苗弱
強則鋤然水渴土苗生二葉則去水以手耘苗弱
用鋤當用鋤苗間細草訖又灌水水每去而不可
宜耘訖灌之苗弱時去苗間細草訖又灌水
處則每耘訖決去水曝根二日後還灌時以手
與苗長半尺許又耘以鋤以苗用鋤耘時以手
早苗長半尺許又耘以鋤
挼軟苗間土面耘至三四度鋤水穀成長唯穊性頗

速不可將熟去水熟還有水則早稻善零隨穀隨
小緩

刈○晚稻水耕正月氷解耕之入糞入土與
今年入土則明年入糞之其地或泥濘

早稻法同糞或入雜草互爲之

或虛浮或水冷則專入新土或莎土塔薄則

布牛馬糞及連枝杵葉乙鄉名加人畫鐽沙亦

佳但爲難得三月上旬至芒種䬃又耕之䬃大抵晚

耕不實種者次之耕者爲上六月內○春

法同三慶耘前三慶耘者不及此者爲下

早不可水耕宜乾耕唯種其法耕訖以檑木

鄉名古打破土塊又以木斫訖鄉名所縱橫擊
音波

平熟治後以稻種一斗和熟糞或尿灰一石為度﨎桃之頹燒為灰用所﨎池尿拌穀秸又足種驅鳥為限苗生苗未成長不可灌水雜草生則雖旱苗橋不可停鋤古語禾鋤頭白有人苗功○苗種法擇水田雖遇旱不乾處二月下旬至三月上旬可耕每水田十分以一分養苗餘九分以擬栽苗橛養苗處并先耕養處如法熟治去水對柳枝軟楷厚布訖足踏之暴土令乾後灌水先漬稻種三日漉入蒿篅空石經一日下種後以板撈鄕名瀧地覆種苗

長一握以上可移栽之先耕苗種處布桴葉
乡名加或牛馬糞臨移栽時又耕之如法熟
治令土極軟每一科栽不過四五苗根未着
土灌水不可令深則此法便於農家之急事也一大旱
○稻種甚多大抵皆同別有一種曰旱稻乡名
偏宜於高地及水冷處然土大燥則不成二
月上旬耕之三月上旬至中旬又耕之作畝
足種訖踏畝背令堅耘時去苗間土勿擁地
若墢薄和熟糞或尿灰種之或旱稻二分稷
二分小豆一分相和兩種歲有水旱九穀隨

歲異壠故交種○若新墾草木茂密處為水則不至全失田者火而耕之三四年後審其土性用糞○若沮澤潤濕荒地則三四月間水草成長時用輪木斲草待土面融熟後下晚稻種又縛柴木兩三箇曳之以牛覆其種至明年可用耒地寶三年則可用牛耕狼省鋤功其輪木之制用堅強木長可四尺為五銳木環以繩繫環令兒童騎椿鞍牛或馬環繩結鞍後橋北鄉名枝兩旁牛馬行則其輪木五銳隅自回轉鉸草破塊若沮甚人牛陷沒

不可入蹢之地用栲撈𢖍鄉各都殺草下種一如前法

種黍粟 附占勿谷粟 青粱粟 蜀黍

三月霜氣頓無 早黍早粟三月上旬晚黍晚粟三月中旬至四月上旬可種 擇良田 粟性宜黑土 細沙高燥不相半者為良下濕不宜

豆稀踪播撒後耕之逐畝左右足踵交踏以足覆土矣

水荏子與黍或粟相和 黍或粟三一分下種茬子長間生雜草與科密處鋤而去之以土壅根鋤至三度勿以無草停鋤待

禾成長兩畝間雜草茂盛用一牛綱其口徐

驅耕之勿致損禾
待十分黃熟可刈
熟糞或尿灰種之糞柔熟易零遇田若塯薄用
又有晚種早熟如青粱郷名
谷擇土厚久陳地種之
五月代草待乾火之灰未冷時
地不至撒擲粟種以鐵齒擺郷音
鋤草省力所出倍常
蕎麥唐麥宜下濕不宜高燥二月早種鋤不
至再而收多

種稷　附姜稷

稷性宜下濕之地二月中旬耕地以木斫{名鄉}

羅{說}熟治自三月上旬至四月上旬皆可種

種法與種黍穄同或撒擲亦得田若塔薄用

糞灰{熟糞與尿灰下澆此}或先布雜草於畝間後耕

種鋤至二度〇稷亦有晚種早熟者{姜鄉名兩}

麥底六月上旬可種

種大豆　小豆　菉豆

大豆小豆種皆有早有晚{早種鄉名春耕晚種鄉名根耕}

{者耕麥根也}早種三月中旬至四月中旬可種也

治田不可過熟下種每科不過三四箇下種淺寡少實然肥田種欲稠則多欲稀薄田種欲稠不宜多鋤不過再鋤田若塉薄用糞灰宜小耕其耕之以擬明年無澤不耕則根也耕耘及收皆與早種同但下種每科四五箇○小豆根耕與大豆根耕同但撒種麥根訖覆耕之一鋤而止○又一法田少者麥未穗時淺耕兩畝間種以大豆收兩麥訖又耕麥根以覆豆根大豆間種秋麥田間種粟皆同此法○用網口牛耕兩畝間

與黍粟田同雜草還茂則再耕之○菉豆薄
田荒地皆可種也稀種一鋤
種大小麥　附春麰
大小麥新舊間接食農家冣急薄田白露節
中田秋分時美田後十日可種大早又不可
則古語曰早種而有節先於五六月間耕之曝陽用木
斫鄕名所摩平下種時又耕之下種訖以鐵
齒擺鄕名羅背訖鄕名羅背所覆種宜厚種早
晚則根深耐寒小明年三月間一鋤之麥根田則
則種則穗耐
依上法菉豆粟木麥根田則預於收穀前用

長柄大鎌及草未黃時刈之積在田畔收穀
訖以其草厚布田上火焚擲種及灰未散耕
之薄田倍加布草如未及刈草用糞又如大
小豆法或於其田先種菉豆或胡麻五六月
間掩耕待草爛後下種時又耕種之如前法
○春夏間刈細柳枝布牛馬廐每五六日取
出積之為盡甚宜於麥○大小麥隨熟隨刈
即輸於場用苫盖覆以防雨作若不及輸
亦須輸運於田畔高處盖覆乘夜輸入暘
以麥薄布場上厚則難乾隨乾隨輾打作名農家

所忙無過於麥古語曰取麥吉語如救火若小遲慢終為災傷○春穬二月間陽氣溫和日可耕盡二月止種法耘法收法與秋麥同種胡麻八鄉名真荏子附油麻者多油
性宜荒地尤良壞四月間雨後則不因雨濕耕地
撒種用擺木鄉名波東乾古破塊覆土鋤不過再隨
熟刈之作束欲小難乾大五六束相倚為叢候
口開逐束倒豎以小杖輕打取了還叢之三
日一打四五遍乃盡若熟田則四月上旬麥
根則趂刈麥後和糞灰稀種○又一法以白

胡麻三分晚小豆一分相和種之或以菉豆二分胡麻一分相和亦得耕訖作䟽以所和種麥科相去一尺

種蕎麥 鄉名木麥

種蕎麥趂時為良 失時遇霜不收 立秋在六月則節前三日內立秋在七月則節後三日內乃其時也宜荒地五月耕之待草爛六月又耕下種時又耕之種子一斗糞灰一石為度 灰漬種小則可田錐塉薄多糞灰則可收其實半黑半白

刈之倒竪則皆黒其早霜慶宜早耕不必待
立秋前後也若山林肥厚之地火耕撒種所
收倍常○漬種法燒牛馬糞為灰以厩池尿
盛貯木槽中漬蕎麥種半日漉出拌灰中令
灰粘著種子

油荏〈本草白油麻唐人謂真荏子〉 水蘇子〈俗謂水荏子〉

農事直説 終

字音義

泡 意囊潤也同穗音逐同 𥠄音秘同 簸去音播揚也 秕音比穀瀝鹿音
濼 也中也 曬乾音礦而音誘不成者穗發者 篤盛音遍草者籍 𣂪雙鑱䤴編也玉具切 甜切徒甘 尿切徒腹少
擺切補 撒散音也散 撈音勞也 劖刺𦈢入洽切 秧音央
泄音曳 買而不鳥藥梯流濁也 塕薄音也 苫編失草廉切 甜切徒
洿水音謂存 耐忍也代切 掭相禾㸃切摩也兩 按如入洽切
㳉音俊伴 杼亦音序 堀切力 秸禾㢱𥝧音切
濘泥音濘 擀音破磨也卧切 㩧以利切乃切 拷音考稂音康
皮切直経伴 梨音翠 敷麥音也年 𨁔水𩲉善切 硻立音也桐
蕎音喬 蜀 𣂪 𨁔 拷秸 擀㩧耐 杼洿泄擺濼泡

APPENDIX A: ORIGINAL TEXT OF CFT AND PHOTOS ... 145

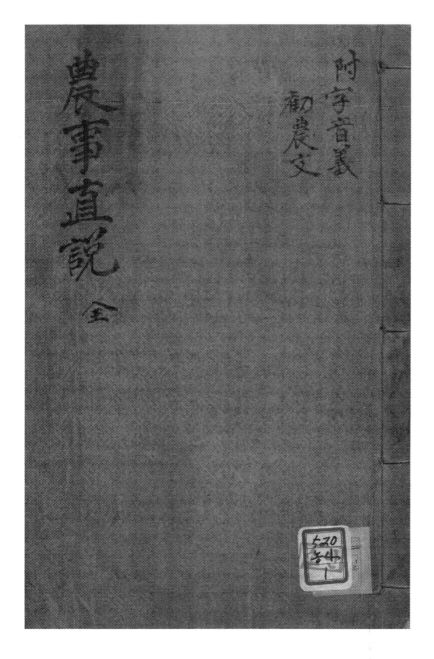

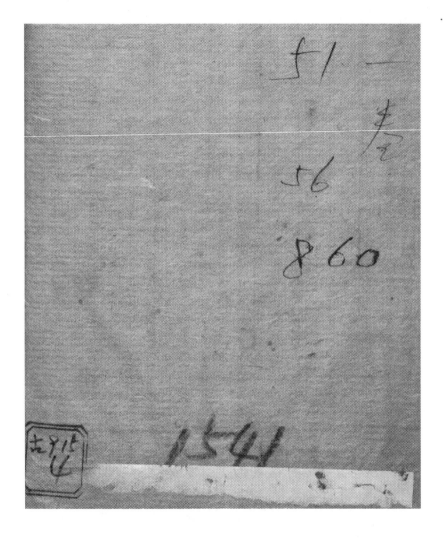

農事直説

○ 備穀種

凡九穀種取堅實不雜不浥者（浥謂鬱浥也種不實則明年穀穗亦不實欲穀揚去秕後沉水去浮者瀝出曝乾以十分無濕氣為度堅藏為尚謂受病於胎也種雜則早晚不等難浥則不生雖生亦不實）

之類（萬葉鄉名空石有欲知來歲所宜以九穀種各一升各盛布囊埋於土宇中（勿令人坐後五十日發取量之最多者其歲所宜也土氣隨地異）

宜二令各異試之（置立春日出之）

○ 冬月以瓮或槽埋置地中要令不凍至臘月多取雪汁盛貯苫

鄉名鹽厚盖古曰䴞䴞之䴞至種時漬種其中泥出晒
乾如此三度或用木槽盛牛馬溺漬種其中
泥出晒乾亦須三度
○耕地
耕地宜徐〻則土軟牛不疲因春夏耕宜淺秋耕宜
深春耕則隨耕隨蓋秋耕則待土色乾白乃治○
旱田初耕後布草燒之又耕則其田自美
○導田耕蒙豆待其茂盛掩耕則不莠不虫變為
良中穊種田之法蒙豆為上小豆胡麻次之五六月
掩殺之為春穀田則畝收十石
○荒田七八月間耕之掩草明年氷釋又耕後下種

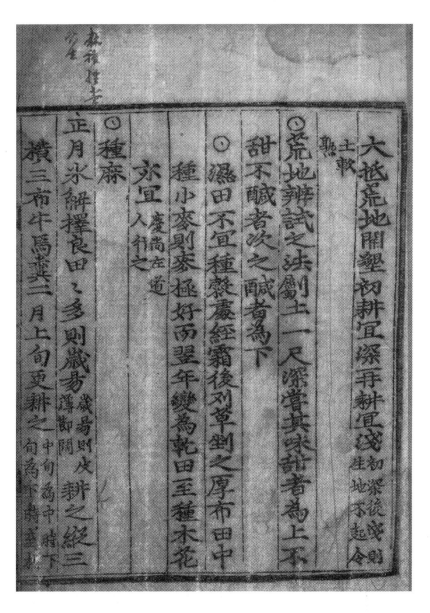

早稻秋收後擇連水源肥膏水田水下可以決去旱 | 稻種有早有晚耕種法有水耕鄉名沙彌又有挿種鄉名冶種除草之法大抵皆同 | 種稻付晚稻 | 種稻忌四季辰戌丑未戌己之日稻種高上寅卯辰月宜戊己四季日 | 之至前後十日內皆可種業 | 上不過一鋤又有晚種吉夏種麻吉日辛巳戊申辛亥巳亥甲申 | 披為其上又布牛馬糞麻長三寸許有雜草則鋤 | 與撒種不均不密不犯用則麻虫撐覆種擴鄉名介松 | 音忽熟治使平後足踏均密撒種又須均須密 | 隨時適恒九度飯熟 | 地上寒氣解便以末所訖羅鄉名所及鐵齒擺

則滲之雨則泌之為上蟒下待水慶次之㷀又耕
雨況肄則苗蔚高慶須兩耕者斷為下矣又耕
之冬月入糞糞或入新土亦得二月上旬又耕之
以水所鄉名所縱橫摩平復以鐵齒擺鄉名手打
破土塊令熟先以稻種漬水經三日漉出納蒿篅
中空石置溫慶頻、開視勿致鬱悒芽長二分均
水田中以板撈㭑鄉名或把撈拼介覆種灌水驅
嚴為以限苗生二葉則去水以手耘鋤然米可用
用鋤當去苗間細草記又灌水灌之苗弱時宜或記
堅鋤則時如川水連通雖旱不渴慶則每莖記快去
宜苗深種苗長半尺許入耘以
水曝根二日後還灌水㷀早稗苗長半尺許入耘以

鋤以曲強鋤可耘時以手接軟苗間土面耘至三四度禾穀長成維賴鋤功且早稻性速不可小緩將熟去水有水則旱稻善乾

零稻隨熟隨刈

晚稻水耕正月氷解耕之入糞入土與早稻法同令入土則明年入糞或入雜草至爲之其地或泥濘或厓浮或水冷則

專入新土或沙土墳薄則布牛馬糞及連枝杼葉鄉名加入糞亦佳爲難但多得三月上旬至芒種

節又耕之大抵節晚耕者不實種者六月望前三度耘者爲上六月內三度耘者次之不及此者爲下鄉名漬種下種覆種灌水耘法

皆與早稻法同晚稻其法耕訖以檀木古音

春旱不可水耕宜乾耕

破打破土塊又以木所鄉名斫
乾𥥞羅
種以稻種一斗和熟糞或尿灰一石為度從橫摩平熟治後
燒地為灰用所剉池尿拌均足種驅烏尿灰作法
未長成不可灌水雜草生則雖旱苗槁不可停鋤
古語云鋤頭自有百本禾
老農亦曰苗知人功
種法擇水田雖遇旱不乾處二月下旬至三月上
旬可耕每水田十分以一分養苗餘九分以擬栽
苗栽養諸幷蒙苗先剉養苗蒙如法熟治去水剉柳枝
較稍厚布訖足踏之曝土令乾後灌水先清稻種
三日漉出入蒿篅鄉名空石經一日下種後以撈櫌名細

麹覆種苗長一握以上可移栽之先耕苗種處布
地乙卿名加或牛馬糞饋移栽時又耕之如法熟
耔築乙草　　　　　　　　　　　　　　　
治令土裡軟每一科栽不過三四苗根未着土灌
水不可令深　曝土時以人跡勘印為度此法便於
　　　　　　種秧掃一大早則伕手農家老事也
下秧吉日　秧同
　　　　　辛未癸酉壬午庚寅癸未甲
己酉乙　　乙巳丙午丁未戊申
卯辛酉總論有　　下五穀種通用
　　　　歲月枝
早稻秧基　日
○以灰和人糞布秧基面假如五斗落多在秧基
則和糞灰三石若初作秧基則和糞灰四石適
中和糞時極細調均若糞塊未破穀着其上反

致浮釀使尚左
道行之胡麻殼坋之牛馬廐賤溜積置
經冬者木綿子和廐灰者亦可右道人行之即可好
麵至於晚稻亦為之
沙當秧基因水下種不能轄乾秧不着根擬待
種而下凡地品不强或因雨水不得如法擇土處
有秧種浮釀之狀則去水如根未着土以沙壅
宜處之根着後貯水
移秧處水若乾涸悉水秘載雨菌弱者儲水秧
基則秧苗自然出水長茂然弱而長移種時不
無拆傷之患矣

○當種或不即移秧有過時䕨點蒙蠋蚼螬蚍蜉
乾草衣菑上焚之後即灌水待其葉間新芽抽
出寸許或量宜長短稻種與趁時揷秧者無
異小灘水焚之無
傷根三日後種之 又種法水田無水雜草荒
蕪未易除處待水取未笛不至損傷東如移
秧者又耕更種一如笛種法則鋤切甚省雖有
水庱人力不足難於除草則亦行此法 䅽䆉䵚
種或云禾不是而老農曰
稻之人皆曰是以穢矣
秋草柳軟枝又眞攃苴以負斫刀下錢
打斷厥下水或人承沾濕或牛馬廐踐蹄和溫

耨耘波倍多中國南京一人[至種五六石之多
者用此法故也然非燥濕任意之處則妙糞行
之凡農家所種或多則鋤功每患過時糞壤亦
難徧及田家之不得多營者良由此也此法最
妙一說小灌水焚
之無會根之患

○種山稻法

稻種甚多大抵皆同別有一種曰旱稻稻山稻徧宜於
高地及水冷處然土太燥則不成二月上旬耕之
三月上旬至中旬又耕之作畝足種訖踏畝背令
堅耘時去苗間土勿擁地蓋墒薄和熟糞或尿灰

APPENDIX A: ORIGINAL TEXT OF CFT AND PHOTOS ... 159

種之或早稻三分稷二分小豆一分相和而種之
雜種之術以歲有水旱九穀適歲異宜故災種則不至全失
若新墾草木茂密處為水田者火而耕之三四年
後審其土性用糞
若沮洳潤瀉荒地則三四月間水草長盛時用輪
木發草待土面融熱後下晚稻種又縛斫木兩三
箇皮之以牛覆其種至明年可用耒地實三年則
可用牛耕 大者鋤 斫生 其輪木之制用堅剛木長可
四尺為五銳隅兩頭黃木環以縄紫環令見童騎
駐鞍牛或馬以繋環縄結鞍後橋 鄉名 扳技 兩傍牛馬

行則其輪木主銳隅自田轉殺草破塊若追入
牛陷沒不可入蹈之地用拷栳鄉名部穀草下種
一如前法

◎種黍粟附占勿谷栗 青粱粟 薥黍 黍忌寅卯
　　　　　　　　　　　　　　　　　丙午日

己酉
戌日

二月霜氣頓無 早黍早粟三月上旬晩黍
　　　　　　粟三月中旬至四月上旬可種
　　　　　　黍先用小豆稀疎播撒粟擇良

田粟細沙性高燥三月相半者爲良地下濕

後耕之逐畝左右足種交蹈以水荏子與黍或粟
已成覆土交運及苗長間生

相和黍或粟子一分下種左右之交

雜草與科密鋤而去之以土擁根鋤至三度勿

以無草停鋤待禾成長兩畝間雜草茂盛用一牛
網其口徐驅耕之勿致損禾土擁禾根泰半熟即
刈栗待十分黃熟可刈 黍熟易零遇風則失後 田若堉薄用
熟糞或尿灰種之 糞或尿灰一石和熟黍苗根時
鋤之則土入苗間仍不成 種黍吉日戊己庚辛
要又有晚種早熟如青粱 動粘生之類者鄉名占
擇土厚久陳地種之 菱林木為上久陳五月伐
草待乾火之灰未冷時地灰冬則蚯蚓至地面
種以鐵齒擺起土覆種鋤草省力而出倍常治田
之法秋耕過冬 間種之粟或因雨澤華節過為
為上粟田尤甚

茂盛則穗而不實綱牛口耕兩畝間搖上水壅節
則更生新根蕘穗長而實
㊀蜀黍鄉名唐黍宜下濕不宜高燥二月早種鋤不至再
種粟吉日丁巳乙卯辛卯三月二卯
而收多　　　　　　　　巳卯巳未種粟為上
㊀種稷附姜䅫　一名穄忌未寅日
稷性宜下濕地二月中旬耕地以木斫熟治自二月
上旬至四月上旬皆可種之法與種黍粟同或撒
擲方得田者塉薄用糞灰也熟漢與煉灰或先布雜
草灰畝間後耕種鋤至二度
㊀稷亥有晚種早熟者鄉名姜䅫兩麥底六月上旬可種

種大豆◦小豆◦菉豆

◦大豆小豆種皆有早有晚根卑種鄉名春㳄晚穫鄉名㳄者耕㴭豕根也 大豆忌卯午丙日亘申子壬好豆同乙

早種三月中旬至四月中旬可種也治田不可過熟下種每科不過三四箇肥田種欲稀薄田種欲稠

綢田若塉薄用糞灰宜少不宜多鋤不過再耕則野不茂

可鋤令葉盡扱之扱訖耕之以擬明年無澤

種豆吉日甲子乙丑壬申丙子戊寅壬午壬寅六月三卯種豆爲上

◦大豆根耕 剗其莖旋耕 耕耘及收皆與早種同但下

種每科四五箇◦小豆根耕與大豆根耕同但撒

種於麥根訖覆耕之一鋤而止◦又一法田少者

兩麥未穗將殘淺耕兩畝間種以大豆狀兩家訖入
耕麥根以覆豆根大豆田間種秋麥麥田間種粟
皆同此法
○用網牛口耕兩畝間與粟田同雜草還茂則尋
一耕之
○菉豆荏田芝荒地皆可種也稀種一鋤撒種方得
稠豆 鄕名 同 藿 五月間種荏田一鋤隨熟摘之
種大小麥附春年大麥忌子丑戌巳小麥同
大小麥新舊間接食農家最惡薄田白露節中田秋
分畔義田後十日可種大早又不可 古語田早種 則虫前有

先於五六月間耕之曝陽用木斫磨平下種時又
耕之下種訖以鐵齒擺或木斫背熟治窊作小畝
畝間和糞灰撒種布熟糞覆種宜厚耐寒甲挐則根深晚種則
穗大明年三月間一鋤之麥根田則依上法秦豆粟
木麥根田則預於收穀前用長柄大鑣及草耰黄
時刈之積在田畔疲穀訖以萬草厚布田上火燎
擲種及灰赤散耕之薄田倍加布草如赤及刈草
用糞灰如大小豆法或於其田先種粟豆或胡麻
五六月間掩耕待草爛後下種時又耕種之如前
法◎種小麥八月上戊為上中戊為中下戊為下

○種大麥八月中戊社前為上下戊為中九月下
捿麥吉日 庚午辛未辛巳 八月三卯為上
庚戌庚子辛亥

○春夏間刈細務枝布中馬礪每五六日取出積之
為薑甚宜於麥
○大小麥隨熟隨刈即收場用笘盖覆以防雨作
若不及輸場亦須輸運於田畔高處盖覆乘夜輸
入遇晴以麥薄布場上 若小麥 厚一寸 別取乾麥隨乾報打報徙名農
家所忙無過於麥 古語曰 慢取麥如救火
春牟二月間陽氣溫和日可耕盖二月止擁法耘
法牧法與秋麥同 叢荷 根登取什註目中即出 麥芒 稻芒 入日中不出者自

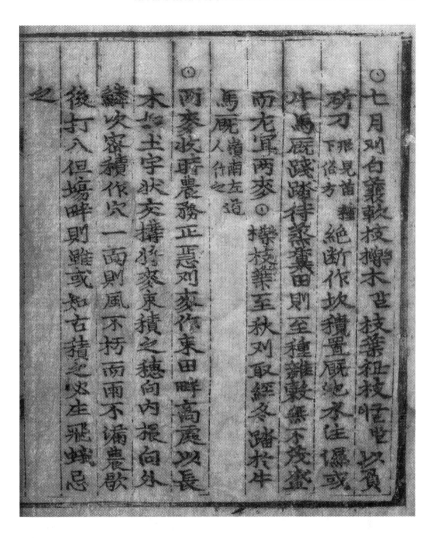

○種胡麻鄉名真荏子擇者多白壤黑者耳曬入藥用不因雨濕耕地撒種用

荏豆荒地亦白壤四月間雨後則不生

檀木破塊覆土鋤不過再隨熟刈之作束欲中大

難五六束相倚為叢候四開遂束倒豎以小炊輕

打敲了還束之三日一打四五遍乃盡者熟田則

四月上旬麥根則起刈麥後和糞灰輥種三月上

旬為上時四月上旬為中時五月上旬為下時月

半前種者多實

○又一法以白胡麻三分晚小豆一分相和種之或

以菉豆二分胡麻一分相和亦得耕訖作畝以所

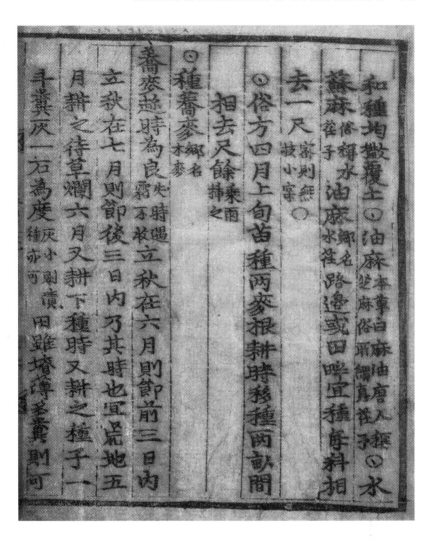

故其實半黑半白刈之倒豎則皆黑其早霜宜早薪不必待立秋前後也弟山林肥厚之地火耕撒種所收倍常

○漬種法燒牛馬糞為灰以厩池水盎貯木槽中漬蕎麥種半日漉出投灰中令灰粘著種子

種木花法 直說下錄

、性宜雜沙燥田二月中旬翻耕三月上旬又耕之以木斫熟治下種時更耕 或二月三日下種種宜頂前下種盖旱耕種立則雖有霜結實如舊綿種先以牛糞授糠以白色盡汶為度多粘承灰傅著乾灰菌大如椽

成畝後播木尖其下端打次畝上隨畝廣狹以
承灰或牛馬糞先行布穴 作穴頗廣 下種無幾 後撒種以
推介掩土 鋤不厭多 待其長成 畝間草淺用一
牛綱口徐々耕之 勿致損傷
世之糞田者 未耕前散糞田中 其功不專於根
莫如此法之為善也
俗人有間種真菁太而不知損害木花 專業
摘花者絕不問種 埋卄陽山仍之
山谷或平原荒田 解水後掘坎 浚胆廣如方席
種子編億時 承灰與牛馬糞填坑 又加新卄綿

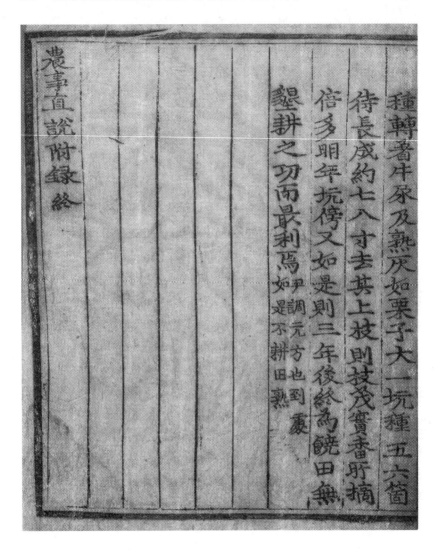

APPENDIX A: ORIGINAL TEXT OF CFT AND PHOTOS ... 173

Appendix B: Farming Tools in CFT and Examples in Other Sources

Hunmin chŏngŭm haerye, 訓民正音解例本 (1446)
Sasŏng tonghae, 四聲通解 (1517)
Hunmong chahoe, 訓蒙字會 (1527)
Hanjŏngnok, 閑情錄 (1618)
Yŏckŏ yuhae, 譯語類解 (1690)
Sallim kyŏngje 山林經濟 (1715)
Revised and Augmented Sallim kyŏngje 增補山林經濟
Mongŏ ryuhae, 蒙語類解 (1768)
Chaemulbo, 才物譜 (1798)
Haedong nongsŏ, 海東農書 (1799)
Sasi ch'anyoch'o, 四時纂要抄 (1655)
Nongga chipsŏng, 農家集成 (1655)

Abbreviation

CFT	Nongsa chiksŏl
CEE	Sasi ch'anyoch'o
CFF	Nongga chipsŏng
HJN	*Hanjŏngnok*
HMCH	*Hunmin chŏngŭm haerye*
STH	*Sasŏng tonghae*

APPENDIX B: FARMING TOOLS IN CFT AND EXAMPLES IN OTHER SOURCES

HMC   Hunmong chahoe
MRH   Mongŏ ryuhae
HDN   Haedong nongsŏ
SLK   Sallim kyŏngje
RASLK   Revised and Augmented Sallim kyŏngje
CMB   Chaemulbo
YYH   Yŏckŏ yuhae
SSC   Sasi ch'anyoch'o

I. *winnowing* 簸箕 *(키, k'i)*
II-1. *A Straw Basket* 蒿篅 鄕名 空石 *(빈섬pinsŏm)*
II-2. *A Straw Bag* 苫薦 鄕名 飛介 *(날개nalgae)*
III. *A Trough-shaped bowl made of wood* 木槽 *(구유kuyu)*
IV. *A Harrow* 木斫, *sohŭlla* (所訖羅)
V. *A Pitchfork* 鐵齒擺 *(쇠스랑syoshiryang* 手愁音)
VI. *A Rake* 撈 曳介 *(끌개 kkŭlgae)*
VII. *A Rake* 板撈 翻地 *(번시 pŏnchi)*
VIII. *A Rake* 把撈 推介 *(밀개 milgae)*
IX. *A Hoe* 鋤 *(호미 hoee)*
X-1. *A Mallet* 樗木 古音波 *(고음파koŭmp'a)*
X-2. *A Tool used to level dirt* 輪木 *(끌개kkŭlgae, oyeu)*
XI. *A Weeder plow* 耒 *(따비 ttabi)*
XII-1. *A Flail* 栲栳 *Rogo* *(도리깨 torikkae)*
XII-2. *A tool to cover the mouth of a horse or cow* 網口
XII-2 *A scythe with a long handle* 長柄大鎌, *(낫 Nat)*

I. 簸箕 *(키, k'i)*
This is pronounced p'a in Sino-Korean. It is a tool used to separate grain from the chaff.

CFT   簸 音播 揚去穗.
HMCH   箕 *Pronounced as k'i.*
MRH   簸箕 *(p'a,k'i).*
STH   簸箕 *k'i.*
HMC   箕 *(k'i, kŭi).*
CMB   揚米器: *A tool that winnows rice,* 箕舌 *(k'i kil): The act of winnowing rice,* 箕踵 (箕後若鞋跟處也 *k'ikkumch'i, k'ikumch'i).*
HDN   東俗通用柳箕: *This refers to a k'i made of bound willow branches.*

II-1. 蒿篅 鄕名 空石 (pinsŏm)

CFT   蒿篅 鄕名空石 音遁草器盛穀者: A basket made of grass (straw) to hold grain.
SLK   藁篅鄕名空石之類: A straw basket made of straw.
YYH   藁薦 (tipchijŭk) 蘆席 (sat): A reed bowl 竹簾: A bamboo bowl.
草簾   A grass bowl.

II-2. 苫薦 鄕名 飛介 (nalgae)

CFT   苫薦 鄕名 飛介: Pronounced "nalgae," this refers to a sŏm of rice for a straw bag. 苫盖 This refers to the straw matting for a straw bag.
CFF   苫草.
SLK   空篅, 苫草, 苫草, 草篅, 藁草, 藁席: The cover for the straw matting of the rice bag.
CMB   藁秸 (kogal) A unsheathed stalk of straw 遷 (音遷收稻具 syŏm): A tool used to harvest rice stalks, pronounced syŏm.

III. 木槽 (kuyu)

This is thought to be a trough-shaped bowl made of wood. The top of a kuyu (trough) is wide and its bottom is narrow. Three long planks are combined and the corners on both ends are blocked. It can be changed at both ends, combined, or taken part. There is no need to carve logs to make one like that in our own country.

CFT   木槽.
HMC   槽: A trough, read as cho in Sino-Korean and malguzi in the vernacular. 槽房 referred to a drinking establishment, 馬槽 referred to malguzi, and 溜槽 was a container that stored rainwater. Kuzi became kui and became today's kuyu.
HJN   槽 Vernacular: kusyu Sino-Korean: cho.
SLK   水槽: kuyu (trough) was transcribed as "木槽" or merely "槽," and very rarely was it transcribed as "水槽."
YYH   馬槽 (malguyu): A malguyu was a trough that could feed three or four horses simultaneously and used in Manchuria and Northern China. A large kuyu that was used to feed two

to three cows at the same time was used in the mountainous areas of Kangwon-do Province.

RASLK 木槽: "水槽" became "木槽," but 木槽 is correct. When transcribed, 木槽 is sometimes written incorrectly as 水槽.

CMB 槽 (*kwiu*).

IV 木斫, 所訖羅 (A harrow)

A mokchak (木斫) was a farming tool used even out of the fields and was pronounced as sohŭlla (所訖羅) in the vernacular. The 木斫 in the Qimin Yaoshu (齊民要術) and Wang Zhen's Nong Shu (農書) is 櫌, that is, a mallet for breaking up dirt clods. This is clearly the same as the 楢木 in CFT. The meaning of the characters in 木斫 is in fact distant from today's harrow as mentioned previously, and this is because the function of this tool as explained in Chinese farming texts is the same as that of a 楢木.

In Yŏngsan, Kyŏngsangnam-do Province, it is called ssŏri or ssŏgŭre, and it used to be called a sohŭre. There are various ssŏre used for dry rice paddies. The same ssŏre is used for normal paddies and can have as many as two to eleven prongs. Ssŏre that have three prongs are all made of wood and the middle prong is either shorter or longer than the rest. Those with eleven teeth are made of iron. They are dragged by cows or donkey and are used as a special farming tool to break up dirt clods or dig up and cover the dirt in dry rice paddies. The Nongzheng quanshu (農政全書) has a picture of this with an explanation attached. However, the same ssŏre in fourteenth-century Nong Shu (農書, 1313) has the yoke open in the front (bottom) and the ssŏre in the rear, while the seventeenth-century Nongzheng quanshu (農政全書, 1639) has the yoke at the top and the ssŏre at the bottom. The picture of the ssŏre does not have a connecting rod and the rope is tied where the main body of the ssŏre and pole meets. It is a particular form of ssŏre. There are a variety of structures and appearances. The ssŏre near Anju (Pyŏngannam-do Province) do not have connecting rods, and the ropes are tied directly to the main body. A tool to level dirt which is used to break up dirt clods. There are seven short iron prongs that are irregularly stuck into the body (a wooden block) with poles at both left and right sides with a H-shaped handle at the end. There is also a clamp fastened in between the body so that the handle can withstand force. This tool is put above dirt clods and then pressed down by the hands and waved left and right to break them. There are various ssŏre used for dry rice paddies. The same ssŏre is used for normal paddies and can have as many as two to eleven prongs. Ssŏre that have three prongs are all made of wood and the middle prong is either shorter or longer than the rest. Those with eleven teeth are made of iron. They are dragged by cows or donkey and are used as a special farming tool to break up dirt clods or dig up and cover the dirt in dry rice paddies.

CFT 木斫 (所訖羅).
SLK 木斫 (*Vernacular name transcribed as sohŭlla*, 所訖羅).
RASLK 所訖羅 (*ssŏhŭre*).
MRH 耙 (*ssŏhŭre*) *Related to the ssŏre, and similar in structure. It is used to break up dirt clods.*
CMB 耙 (*ssŏhŭre*) *This refers to what is known as a ssŏre today, or harrow.*
HDN 秒 (*ssŏŭre*): *Vernacular: ssyŏŭre Sino-Korean: ch'yo*).

V. 鐵齒擺 手愁音 (A pitchfork)

This is defined as an "iron syoshiryang" but it is different from the soesŭrang. The ones used in Northern China and Manchuria have long prongs (within 15 cm), which can be over ten in number. 鐵齒擺 is the Chinese transcription of soesŭrang (a pitchfork). Soesŭrang is listed as syoshirang in HMC. *Soshirang has three prongs, but a Chinese pitchfork has four to six. Therefore, the efficiency and convenience of a soshirang are comparable to its Chinese counterpart. However, it is far better than its Japanese counterpart, which only has two prongs.*

CFT 鐵齒擺 (*susuŭm*).
HMC 耙 (*Vernacular name: sŏhŭrae Sino-Korean: p'a, also known as soeshiryang in the vernacular*).
SLK 鐵齒擺 (*susuŭm*).
YYH 鐵杷子 (*An iron syoshiryang*): *A leveling tool.*
RASLK 鐵齒鈀 (*soshirang*).

VI. 捞 曳介 (A kkŭlgae rake)

CFT 捞 (*yegae*): 捞 (*No*) was a type of rake that was widely used by farmers. Long pine branches would be tied together at one end and loaded with a rock. This would then be dragged over sown fields to cover up the seeds with dirt, and sometimes a child was used as a weight on the branches instead of a rock. This was also called a "kaeji" in Pyŏngan-do

Province, and after cutting pine branches to 50~60 cm in length, an appropriate-sized rock would be tied to the branches and straw would be coiled around the rock and branches. After sowing was complete, the part where the rock and straw touched would rub against the dirt and the pine needles would cover the seeds with dirt. Women would follow behind wearing straw shoes to stamp down the earth. This was used in many counties in western Kyŏnggi Province that faced the ocean. Round pine logs would be linked together and mounted with short prongs. It was usually dragged by cows. This was dragged by a person when it was used to plow and level the fields, weeding and planting rice when the clay earth would dry out, or when planting and covering up the rice plants with dirt. If more force was needed, it was loaded with grass or a rock. Kkŭlgae: A wide wooden block would be threaded with rope, which would then be dragged. This was called a kkŭlgae or kkŭnggae in Kyŏngsang Province. It is also described as "used to break the sand on the surface of salt fields." This was used in many counties in western Kyŏnggi Province that faced the ocean. Round pine logs would be linked together and mounted with short prongs. It was usually dragged by cows. This was dragged by a person when it was used to plow and level the fields, weeding and planting rice when the clay earth would dry out, or when planting and covering up the rice plants with dirt. If more force was needed, it was loaded with grass or a rock. Kkŭlgae: A wide wooden block would be threaded with rope, which would then be dragged. This was called a kkŭlgae or kkŭnggae in Kyŏngsang Province. It is also described as "used to break the sand on the surface of salt fields."

Also, a round and long club mounted evenly with tree branches with leaves would be used to cover up fields with hemp seeds, and this was called a noja (捞子).

CEE　　捞: *Kkŭlgae.* 把捞 is another variety of this tool.
SLK　　捞.
RASLK　曳捞.

VII. 板捞 (翻地) A pŏnchi rake
CFT 板捞 (pŏnchi): The vernacular name for this is pŏnji. Pŏn means turn over inside which is lubricity. It has no fixed size, but generally is an oblong wooden board 2.5 m long and about 30 cm high. It is usually inside part tied to the prongs of a ssŏre and dragged by cows, but

humans also dragged it from both sides. Nowadays, they are frequently used to level out rice seedbeds, but they were also used to cover up the rice seeds with dirt in the fifteenth century. Leveling out the earth with this was called "pŏnji ch'inda" in Kyŏnggi Province. A long plank with a rope attached. The explanation and picture of this tool have been transferring directly from Nong Shu. A pŏnchi, transcribed as 板撈 in CFT and farm management, is also transcribed as 板橯 in CMB. However, the author did not take this into consideration and instead appropriated the name directly from Nong Shu. In Nong Shu, it is shown with a handle tied to an oblong plank.

SLK　　　板撈 (pŏchi).
RASLK　　板橯.
CMB　　　板橯 (pŏnchi): *A tool to level dirt*→板撈 *in CFT*.
HDN　　　平板 (pŏnchi).
CMB　　　平板: 板橯 *is said to be the same as pŏnchi*.

VIII. 把撈 (推介) A milgae rake
CFT 把撈 (推介): *A milgae* (推介) can be seen as a kind of rake that is used today to cover up seeds. This was called a milgae in Kangwŏn-do Province and a mirae in Changhŭng, Chŏlla-do Province, but the former of these names is correct. Although rakes push or drag dirt, this tool is thus named for pushing dirt. In addition, this was called a ttaenggilgae in Bongyang, Ch'ungch'ŏnbuk Province, a tanggŭrae in Yŏngsan, Kyŏngsangnam Province and Dŏkjŏkdo in Kyŏnggi Province, and tanggŭlgae in Kŏmundo, Chŏllanam Province. These names all come from the fact that these rakes dragged dirt.

SLK　　　把撈 (椎介): *Although the name of a* 把撈 *was transcribed as* 椎介, *this is an error in transcribing* 推介. *It is written as* "推介" *in CFT*.
RASLK　　把橯: 撈 *is changed to* 橯 *in farm management*.

IX. 鋤 (A hoe)
CFT 鋤: *Vernacular: homi, Sino-Korean: sŏ, a small hoe,* 鋤: *Hoe*. This was transcribed as 鉏 or 鋤 in the fifteenth century. "*A hoe is the most widely used traditional farming tool....they are generally categorized for use in*

fields or paddies. The ones used for paddies have short handles, while the ones used for fields have long handles. The former have triangle shaped blades with sharp ends and dig deep into the dirt to uproot grass. The latter have blades with flat ends and are convenient for scraping weeds on the surface."

With a 立鋤, there is no inconvenience of having to bend over to remove weeds. "As our hoes have very short poles, they must be used while sitting down in dry or wet fields." However, this does not mean that hoes with long poles did not exist. As Bak Chega explains in Discourse on Northern Learning, he says, "It is two and a half cha long and its neck is one cha long." Therefore, a hoe could be used standing up.

The hoe in HDN has a long tang in comparison with the handle, and the blade at the end of the tang is bent nearly at a right angle. Also, the length of the blade is much longer than its rear and the end of the blade is pointed. Thus, this sort of hoe is appropriate for use in the fields and is quite similar to the sickle-shaped hoe used in the south of Yŏngnam or Honam and in Jeju.

耨 (耘田器): The Nongzheng quanshu states, "The Lüshi Chunqiu says its pole is one cha long in order so that it may be used appropriately, and is six ch'on wide in order that it may fit in between the grains."

農具六則 changes 立鋤 to 長柄鋤 and says "Its pole is two and a half cha in length and its neck is one cha long. Its blade is shaped like the leaf of a large kudzu, bending inwards. It is proper to use this standing up." It also says, "If sprouts appear, this is used to scrape the dirt of the levees while standing up and remove and bury the weeds on the left and right; this then naturally benefits the roots." 小鋤: "In the past, after plowing was done, then a 小鋤 was used to scrape the levees and small pits were made in which seeds were planted." 短柄鋤 is presumed to be similar to a hoe. 櫌鋤: Both 耨 and 櫌鋤 are tools used to harvest crops. The production method of these tools was seen while passing through Liaodong and Hebei. The blade resembles a kudzu leaf and the neck is one cha and the pole is over two cha. This can be used while standing. *A hoe's blade resembles a triangle and is quite long, up to 15~20 cm.*

HMCH *Homae* (鉏).
SSC   鉏.
HMC   鋤, 钁 (*Vernacular: homae, Sino-Korean: hwak, a large hoe*).
HJN   鋤.
SLK   鉏,鋤.
YYH   鋤子: *A weeding tool. Homŭi is the transcription of hoe.*

APPENDIX B: FARMING TOOLS IN CFT AND EXAMPLES IN OTHER SOURCES   183

RASLK   鋤子.
MRH   鋤子 (homŭi).
CMB   鋤 (耘田器 homae) 钁 (大鋤) 耨 (耘田器): The Nongzheng quanshu states, "The Lüshi Chunqiu says its pole is one cha long in order so that it may be used appropriately, and is six ch'on wide in order that it may fit in between the grains."
HDN   鋤 (homae):

X-1. 檑木 古音波 (A mallet Vernacular name: koŭmp'a)
CFT 檑木 (koŭmp'a) "곰방메" "곰베," "곤븨". A 檑木 is used to break up dirt clods and it was called koŭmp'a as stated earlier and it thought to have evolved into kombangme. This is a round wooden block 30 cm in length and 5–10 cm in diameter with a long piece of wood stuck into it. This tool is called different names according to region, such as t'onggombae in Ch'ungch'ŏng-do Province. They are used to break up dirt clods and were called koŭmp'a, which then became today's kombangme. This has a round wooden block (30 cm long and 5–10 cm in diameter) with a long handle and is called a t'onggombae in Ch'ungch'ŏngbuk-do Province, pungt'unggombae in Kyŏngsangnam Province, and kombaengi in Chŏllanam-do Province. A tool used to break up dirt clods, a kombangme 無齒杷, 机 (komire) komurae, 樺 (kkŭŭgae) kkŭlgae, 欀 kombangme a small mallet for breaking dirt cods, 刮板 narae a ssŏre without prongs.

SSC   檑木: This refers to a mallet as stated in CFT.
SLK   檑木 (koŭmp'a).

X-2. 輪木 yunmok, kkŭlgae, 목작배, 써레등, 끌개
CFT   輪木 This kills the grass in low wetlands and breaks up dirt clods. A tool used to level dirt.
CFT   縛柴木兩參箇 pakshimokyangsamgae Made from three or four pieces of split wood tied together, kkŭlgae - A tool used to level dirt which is used for children to ride sleighs dragged by cows.
CFT   木斫背 mokchakpae, ssŏraetŭng, kkŭlgae – A tool used to level dirt.
SSC   捞 kkŭlgae.
STH   碌碡 ryuktok Is shaped like a roller.
HMC   Ssŏre, pŏnji, tolt'ae, soesŭrang.

XI. 耒 Sino-Korean: roe Vernacular: ttabi (a weeder plow)

CFT   *17 Sino-Korean: roe Vernacular: ttabi A weeder plow, a supplement to a plow – a plowing tool.*
SSC   犁 *ri A plow.*
STH   犁 *po Another name for a plow,* 枚 *(hŏm) Karae, sap (shovels).*
HMC   *Po, ttabi, karae (shovel), sap (shovel).*
SLK   犁 *Plow, light plow,* 胡犁 *Light plow.*
RASLK   耒耟 *roegŏ A plow.*
CMB   踏犁 *tapri A plow,* 耒 *A ttabi handle,* 粗 *A ttabi blade.*

XII-1. 栲栳 Rogo in Sino-Korean, refers to a flail (torikkae)

CFT   栲栳 *rogo, torikkae – A threshing tool, a smaller torikkae with three or four twigs attached to the end of the rod.*
STH   枷 *torich'ae (torikkae).*
HMC   *torich'ae (torikkae).*
CMB   枷 *torikkae.*
HDN   連枷 *torikkae A handle used to spin the torikkae.*
稻床 *A log threshing stand. A tool used to beat grain, and a tool used by rich farmers.*
稻箸 *A threshing comb to separate the grain from chaff; made from iron chopsticks.*

XII-2. 網口 A tool to cover the mouth of a horse or cow

CFT   網口 *A net to cover a horse's or cow's mouth – other such tools.*
CMB   篼子 *A net to cover the mouth.*

XII-2. 長柄大鎌 A scythe with a long handle Nat

CFT   *21* 長柄大鎌 *A scythe with a long handle – a harvesting tool.*
HMCH   鎌 *Nat.*
SSC   柴鎌 *Sikshikyŏm. A curved sickle used to cut wood.*
HMC   *A sickle* 鎌, 釤, 鍥, 銍.
CMB   鎺鏺 *(kwagyŏl)* 鏺栗鋻 *(palyŏlgyŏn) A cutting blade, a type of sickle,* 銍 *A short sickle used to cut grain,* 釤 *A large sickle.*
HDN   鎌 *A sickle.*

Appendix C: Geographical Appendix of the Veritable Records of King Sejong (世宗實錄地理志) GAVK

Household (戶), Population (口), Arable Land (墾田), Wet Field (水田), Dry Field (旱田), Ratio (分).

Table C.1 Triple types of information: Household, Adult male population, Arable land unit 結 (Myŏck)

Kyŏnggi province		Households	Adult male population	Arable land unit: Myŏck (結)	Ratio of wet field	Wetfield unit: Myŏck (結)	Dryfield unit: Myŏck (結)	The ratio of wet field (%)
Kanghwa	江華	2445	3283	5606	1/2	2803	2803	50.00
Suwŏn	水原	1842	4926	19,154	1/2	9577	9577	50.00
Yangchu	楊州	1481	2726	15,190	3/10	4557	10,633	30.00
Kwangchu	廣州	1436	3110	16,269	1/4	4067	12,202	25.00
Yichŏn	利川	1026	3898	7532	1/2	3766	3766	50.00
Haepung	海豐	792	1381	6564	1/2	3282	3282	50.00
Koyang	高陽	679	1314	6326	1/2	3163	3163	50.00
Kyoha	交河	590	1629	3956	4/7	2261	1695	57.14
Yohŭng	驪興	538	1144	6145	1/2	3073	3073	50.00
Wŏnpyŏng	原平	494	1316	5325	2/5	2130	3195	40.00
Namyang	南陽	487	778	4348	3/8	1631	2718	37.50
T'ongchin	通津	458	971	5361	1/2	2681	2681	50.00
Yongin	龍仁	457	1168	5988	3/8	2246	3743	37.50
Pupyŏng	富平	429	954	5296	1/2	2648	2648	50.00
Yangsŏng	陽城	425	1210	4742	1/2	2371	2371	50.00
Ansŏng	安城	424	1763	5436	1/2	2718	2718	50.00
Ch'ollyŏng	川寧	413	1234	4573	1/4	1143	3430	25.00
Ŭmchuk	陰竹	390	1088	3163	1/2	1582	1582	50.00
Yanggŭn	楊根	388	1686	4343	1/6	724	3619	16.67
P'ochŏn	抱川	371	1222	3948	1/4	987	2961	25.00
Yimgang	臨江	364	878	3934	1/5	787	3147	20.00
Inchŏn	仁川	357	1412	2601	3/7	1115	1486	42.86
Ch'ŏlwŏn	鐵原	351	770	4343	1/4	1086	3257	25.00
Yangchi	陽智	346	609	2068	1/2	1034	1034	50.00
Kŭmchŏn	衿川	327	937	2762	2/5	1105	1657	40.00
K'impo	金浦	318	651	3032	1/2	1516	1516	50.00

(continued)

Table C.1 (continued)

Kyŏnggi province		Households	Adult male population	Arable land unit: Myŏck (結)	Ratio of wet field	Wetfield unit: Myŏck (結)	Dryfield unit: Myŏck (結)	The ratio of wet field (%)
Ansan	安山	302	588	2289		763	1526	33.33
Kapyŏng	加平	288	987	3057				
Yimchin	臨津	274	613	2571	1/2	1286	1286	50.00
Chipyŏng	砥平	267	515	3335	1/5	667	2668	20.00
Kwachŏn	果川	244	743	3128	1/3	1043	2085	33.33
SakRyŏng	朔寧	233	722	3854				
Yangchŏn	楊川	222	509	1877	1/3	626	1251	33.33
Chinwi	振威	221	535	2841	1/2	1421	1421	50.00
Kyotong	喬桐	221	562	1986	2/3	1324	662	66.67
Chŏksŏng	積城	212	380	2663	1/5	533	2130	20.00
Yŏnch'ŏn	漣川	186	360	1939	2/9	431	1508	22.22
Changtan	長湍	170	467	1645	1/3	548	1097	33.33
Machŏn	麻田	146	484	1171	1/4	293	878	25.00
Anhyŏp	安峽	140	410	1422				
Yŏngp'ŏng	永平	138	419	2487	1/8	311	2176	12.50
		20,892	50,352	194,270				

Chungch'ŏng province		Households	Population	Arable land unit: Myŏck (結)	Ratio of wet field	Wetfield (Kyŏl)	Dryfield (Kyŏl)	The ratio of wet field (%)
Kongchu	公州	2167	10,049	18,526	3/8	6947	11,579	37.50
Ch'ungchu	忠州	1871	7452	19,893	3/10	5968	13,925	30.00
Ch'ŏngchu	清州	1589	6738	18,193	1/3	6064	12,129	33.33
Hongchu	洪州	1379	6031	11,386	1/2	5693	5693	50.00
Tŏksan	德山	649	3214	5199	5/9	2888	2311	55.56
Okch'ŏn	沃川	558	1834	4178	1/4	1045	3134	25.00

(continued)

Table C.1 (continued)

Chungch'ŏng province		Households	Population	Arable land unit: Myŏck (結)	Ratio of wet field	Wetfield (Kyŏl)	Dryfield (Kyŏl)	The ratio of wet field (%)
Chiksan	稷山	553	2111	5446	1/2	2723	2723	50.00
Chinchŏn	鎭川	550	1923	6599	3/4	4949	1650	75.00
Ch'ŏnan	天安	506	2385	5158	1/2	2579	2579	50.00
Ŭnchin	恩津	506	1717	4207	1/2	2104	2104	50.00
Sŏsan	瑞山	489	1887	7283	2/5	2913	4370	40.00
Asan	牙山	482	1822	6566	1/2	3283	3283	50.00
Chuksan	竹山	470	2118	5789	4/9	2573	3216	44.44
Yimchŏn	林川	460		4624	1/2	2312	2312	50.00
Koesan	槐山	445	1303	3880	1/4	970	2910	25.00
Sŏch'ŏn	舒川	421	1876	3774	3/5	2264	1510	60.00
Chechŏn	堤川	415	1235	3915	1/7	559	3356	14.29
Myŏnch'ŏn	沔川	405	3155	4053	4/9	1801	2252	44.44
Mokch'ŏn	木川	404	2186	3017	2/5	1207	1810	40.00
Sŏksŏng	石城	395	1208	2449	1/2	1225	1225	50.00
Taehŭng	大興	388	1518	3026	1/3	1009	2017	33.33
Nisan	尼山	384	1591	3787	5/9	2104	1683	55.56
Buyŏ	扶餘	382	1337	3762	1/3	1254	2508	33.33
Yŏnsan	連山	378	1487	3836	3/7	1644	2192	42.86
Poryŏng	保寧	365	1213	3127	4/9	1390	1737	44.44
Munŭi	文義	353	1871	2754	1/3	918	1836	33.33
Yŏngi	燕岐	348	1446	2916	2/5	1166	1750	40.00
Hongsan	洪山	348	1971	3385	1/2	1693	1693	50.00
Onsu	溫水	343	1516	3853	1/3	1284	2569	33.33
Hansan	韓山	342	1607	3060	3/5	1836	1224	60.00
Sinch'ang	新昌	338	1555	3064	1/2	1532	1532	50.00

(continued)

Table C.1 (continued)

Chungch'ŏng province		Households	Population	Arable land unit: Mwŏck (結)	Ratio of wet field	Wetfield (Kyŏl)	Dryfield (Kyŏl)	The ratio of wet field (%)
Poŭn	報恩	327	1457	5229	1/3	1743	3486	33.33
Yesan	禮山	321	1477	3732	3/7	1599	2133	42.86
Hwanggan	黃澗	308	742	1725	1/2	863	863	50.00
Kyelsŏng	結城	304	1698	3251	1/3	1084	2167	33.33
Hoedŏk	懷德	300	1266	2688	2/5	1075	1613	40.00
Ch'ŏngan	清安	293	1419	3334	2/7	953	2381	28.57
Tangchin	唐津	284	1489	2632	3/4	1974	658	75.00
Chŏngyang	青陽	265	1021	2559	2/5	1024	1535	40.00
Chŏngsan	定山	258	1113	2277	1/3	759	1518	33.33
Haemi	海美	258	855	2763	3/7	1184	1579	42.86
Tanyang	丹陽	235	724	1169		112	1057	9.58
Ch'ŏngsan	青山	235	607	1573		289	1284	18.37
Yŏngdong	永同	227	951	2592	1/6	432	2160	16.67
Yŏngch'un	永春	195	582	1198		21	1177	1.75
Ch'ŏngp'ung	清風	191	656	1955		135	1820	6.91
Nanmp'o	藍浦	180	949	2686	1/2	1343	1343	50.00
P'yŏngt'aek	平澤	179	704	2234	3/5	1340	894	60.00
T'aean	泰安	173	547	2985	2/7	853	2132	28.57
Ŭmsŏng	陰城	171	726	1993	3/10	598	1395	30.00
Chŏnŭi	全義	166	572	1575	1/4	394	1181	25.00
Piin	庇仁	166	651	1622	1/3	541	1081	33.33
Chincham	鎭岑	153	583	1480	1/2	740	740	50.00
Hoein	懷仁	146	633	1146	1/9	127	1019	11.11
Yŏnp'ung	延豐	143	341	1011	1/9	112	899	11.11

(continued)

Table C.1 (continued)

kyŏngsang province		Households	Population	Arable land unit: Myŏck (結)	Ratio of wet field	Wetfield (Kyŏl)	Dryfield (Kyŏl)	The ratio of wet field (%)
Sangchu	尙州	1845	3132	15,360	2/5	6144	9216	40.00
Chinchu	晉州	1628	5906	12,730	1/2	6365	6365	50.00
Milyang	密陽	1612	5522	10,285	1/3	3428	6857	33.33
Kyŏngchu	慶州	1552	5894	19,733	3/8	7400	12,333	37.50
Sŏngchu	星州	1479	5807	15,555	3/8	5833	9722	37.50
Kimhae	金海	1290	6642	7809	1/2	3905	3905	50.00
Ch'angwŏn	昌原	1094	4955	4663	1/2	2332	2332	50.00
Ulsan	蔚山	1058	4161	6482	4/9	2881	3601	44.44
Yŏngch'ŏn	永川	863	3672	7432	2/5	2973	4459	40.00
Andong	安東	847	3320	11,283	2/7	3224	8059	28.57
Ch'angryŏng	昌寧	825	4352	4846	1/3	1615	3231	33.33
Sŏnsan	善山	809	4218	9170	2/3	6113	3057	66.67
Yŏch'ŏn	醴泉	781	3800	7298	3/8	2737	4561	37.50
Haman	咸安	732	3266	3976	1/3	1325	2651	33.33
Chŏngdo	淸道	649	3361	3932	1/3	1311	2621	33.33
Ŭisŏng	義城	637	1955	5068	1/5	1014	4054	20.00
Kŭsan	金山	533	2064	4673	3/8	1752	2921	37.50
Kaeryŏng	開寧	531	2359	4190	2/5	1676	2514	40.00
Kosŏng	固城	531	2885	3941	1/2	1971	1971	50.00
Kŏch'ang	居昌	505	1640	3423	1/2	1712	1712	50.00
Ŭiryŏng	宜寧	504	1629	3558	2/3	2372	1186	66.67
Anŭm	安陰	481	793	1793	1/2	897	897	50.00
Hyŏnpung	玄風	477	1871	3625	2/7	1036	2589	28.57
hyŏpch'ŏn	陜川	464	1517	2975	2/5	1190	1785	40.00
Chogye	草溪	463	2537	2568	3/10	770	1798	30.00
Taegu	大丘	436	1329	6543	3/10	1963	4580	30.00

(continued)

Table C.1 (continued)

kyŏngsang province		Households	Population	Arable land unit: Myŏck (結)	Ratio of wet field	Wetfield (Kyŏl)	Dryfield (Kyŏl)	The ratio of wet field (%)
Hamyang	咸陽	428	1948	2473	1/2	1237	1237	50.00
Yangsan	梁山	425	937	2030	4/9	902	1128	44.44
Hŭnghae	興海	423	1885	1913	5/9	1063	850	55.56
Ŏnyang	彥陽	421	1458	1518	1/2	759	759	50.00
Yŏngil	迎日	417	1742	2106	2/5	842	1264	40.00
Yonggung	龍宮	396	2125	4191	1/3	1397	2794	33.33
Sinnyŏng	新寧	382	1301	2047	3/10	614	1433	30.00
Yŏngch'ŏn	榮川	377	3087	4118	1/3	1373	2745	33.33
Sach'ŏn	泗川	370	1817	2077	1/2	1039	1039	50.00
Hamch'ang	咸昌	368	2140	2929	3/7	1255	1674	42.86
Hadong	河東	346	1108	1272	2/3	848	424	66.67
Ch'ilwŏn	漆原	337	1331	1819	1/4	455	1364	25.00
Indong	仁同	320	1086	3345	3/10	1004	2342	30.00
kyŏngsang Province	慶山	318	1337	3479	3/8	1305	2174	37.50
Ŭihŭng	義興	307	955	1830	1/3	610	1220	33.33
Samga	三嘉	307	2027	1913	1/2	957	957	50.00
Tongrae	東萊	290	1151	1723	5/8	1077	646	62.50
Koryŏng	高靈	287	1722	2177	2/5	871	1306	40.00
Yŏngdŏk	盈德	286	1110	1246	1/7	178	1068	14.29
Sunhŭng	順興	284	1679	2459	3/7	1054	1405	42.86
Kunwi	軍威	284	677	2208	1/3	736	1472	33.33
Konnam	昆南	271	1300	1824	1/2	912	912	50.00
Pian	比安	266	1102	2675	3/10	803	1873	30.00
Mungyŏng	聞慶	261	1065	2789	1/5	558	2231	20.00
Yŏngsan	靈山	257	1134	3001	3/10	900	2101	30.00

(continued)

Table C.1 (continued)

Kyŏngsang province		Households	Population	Arable land unit: Myŏck (結)	Ratio of wet field	Wetfield (Kyŏl)	Dryfield (Kyŏl)	The ratio of wet field (%)
Sanŭm	山陰	257	1138	1535	3/7	658	877	42.86
Ponghwa	奉化	243	473	1006	1/5	201	805	20.00
Ch'ŏngha	清河	235	724	799	1/3	266	533	33.33
Chinsŏng	珍城	234	872	1750	4/7	1000	750	57.14
Chirye	知禮	230	1200	1138	1/3	379	759	33.33
Yŏnghae	鴬海	215	1538	2720	1/7	389	2331	14.29
Changgi	長鬐	203	813	1264	1/4	316	948	25.00
Chinhae	鎭海	202	953	765	3/7	328	437	42.86
Hayang	河陽	177	1087	2216	1/3	739	1477	33.33
Kichang	機張	174	397	730	1/2	365	365	50.00
Yean	禮安	174	749	908	1/8	114	795	12.50
Kich'ŏn	基川	160	709	1633	1/2	817	817	50.00
Kŏche	巨濟	153	423	709	1/2	355	355	50.00
Chinbo	眞寶	78	526	877		82	795	9.35
Ch'ŏngsong	靑松	36	217	1315		115	1200	8.75

Chŏlla province		Households	Population	Arable land unit: Myŏck (結)	Ratio of wet field	Wetfield (Kyŏl)	Dryfield (Kyŏl)	The ratio of wet field (%)
Cheju	濟州	5207	8324	3977				
Chŏnchu	全州	1565	5829	18,664	1/2	9332	9332	50.00
Taechŏng	大靜	1357	8500	2227				
Namwŏn	南原	1300	4912	12,508	1/2	6254	6254	50.00
Nachu	羅州	1089	4026	15,339	1/2	7670	7670	50.00
Muchin	茂珍	860	4182	10,880	1/2	5440	5440	50.00
Chŏngŭi	旌義	685	2073	3208				

(continued)

Table C.1 (continued)

Chŏlla province		Households	Population	Arable land unit: Myŏck (結)	Ratio of wet field	Wetfield (Kyŏl)	Dryfield (Kyŏl)	The ratio of wet field (%)
Sunchŏn	順天	467	2618	7315	1/2	3658	3658	50.00
Kŭmsan	錦山	452	1890	3952	1/3	1317	2635	33.33
Kimche	金堤	409	2065	7281	5/8	4551	2730	62.50
Imp'i	臨陂	396	1949	6447	7/10	4513	1934	70.00
Kobu	古阜	357	1592	6601	5/9	3667	2934	55.56
Muchang	茂長	356	2033	5895	2/5	2358	3537	40.00
Kangchin	康津	355	1644	7179	1/2	3590	3590	50.00
Tamyang	潭陽	346	1760	5852	1/2	2926	2926	50.00
Yŏngam	靈巖	333	1229	6504	5/9	3613	2891	55.56
Yŏnggwang	靈光	331	2137	9604	1/2	4802	4802	50.00
Puan	扶安	323	1662	7140	5/9	3967	3173	55.56
Changsu	長水	320	812	1773	2/9	394	1379	22.22
Iksan	益山	319	1623	3726	3/7	1597	2129	42.86
Sunch'ang	淳昌	317	1092	5724	2/5	2290	3434	40.00
Hamp'yŏng	咸平	315	1608	6487	2/5	2595	3892	40.00
Muan	務安	315	1030	4020	5/9	2233	1787	55.56
Yŏsan	礪山	312	1419	4362	4/7	2493	1869	57.14
Nakan	樂安	306	1439	2016	1/2	1008	1008	50.00
Hamyŏl	咸悅	288	1384	3298	5/8	2061	1237	62.50
Changhŭng	長興	276	1041	6124	2/5	2450	3674	40.00
Kŭmgu	金溝	262	1207	3729	3/5	2237	1492	60.00
Kosan	高山	260	2028	3116	1/6	519	2597	16.67
Okgu	沃溝	257	1194	4444	7/10	3111	1333	70.00
Posŏng	寶城	253	1245	5233	3/5	3140	2093	60.00
T'aein	泰仁	247	1526	5304	1/2	2652	2652	50.00
Nampyŏng	南平	236	1333	5105	3/7	2188	2917	42.86

(continued)

194   APPENDIX C: GEOGRAPHICAL APPENDIX …

Table C.1 (continued)

Chŏlla province		Households	Population	Arable land unit: Myŏck (結)	Ratio of wet field	Wetfield (Kyŏl)	Dryfield (Kyŏl)	The ratio of wet field (%)
Kwangyang	光陽	228	1220	2010	1/2	1005	1005	50.00
Ch'angpyŏng	昌平	219	952	2577	1/2	1289	1289	50.00
Hŭngdŏk	興德	216	1051	3134	1/2	1567	1567	50.00
Hwasun	和順	209	615	1247	2/5	499	748	40.00
Yongan	龍安	190	662	1991	2/7	569	1422	28.57
Changsŏng	長城	183	840	3366	3/8	1262	2104	37.50
Mangyŏng	萬頃	172	727	3508	7/10	2456	1052	70.00
Muchu	茂朱	172	715	1501	1/4	375	1126	25.00
Chinan	鎭安	169	722	2772	2/5	1109	1663	40.00
Kochang	高敞	164	974	2235	1/2	1118	1118	50.00
Kohŭng	高興	157	686	2156	1/2	1078	1078	50.00
K'oksŏng	谷城	148	657	2353	1/2	1177	1177	50.00
Chinwŏn	珍原	144	747	2340	5/9	1300	1040	55.56
Unbong	雲峯	139	551	1796	1/2	898	898	50.00
Nŭngsŏng	綾城	139	763	3229	3/7	1384	1845	42.86
Imsil	任實	138	803	5392	2/9	1198	4194	22.22
Kurye	求禮	137	677	1735	1/2	868	868	50.00
Okgwa	玉果	136	837	2573	3/8	965	1608	37.50
Chŏngŭp	井邑	130	858	2658	3/5	1595	1063	60.00
Haechin	海珍	122	707	5941	2/5	2376	3565	40.00
Chinsan	鎭山	114	154	1207	1/10	121	1086	10.00
Tongbok	同福	90	289	1662	1/3	554	1108	33.33
Yongdam	龍潭	86	274	1851	1/9	206	1645	11.11

(continued)

Table C.1 (continued)

Hwanghae province		Households	Population	Arable land unit: Myŏck (結)	Ratio of wet field	Wetfield (Kyŏl)	Dryfield (Kyŏl)	The ratio of wet field (%)
Kangryŏng	康翎	389	1068	3108	1/7	444	2664	14.29
Kangŭm	江陰	374	964	3499	1/6	583	2916	16.67
Koksan	谷山	816	2828	6726		54	6672	0.80
Munhwa	文化	950	2136	7185	1/5	1437	5748	20.00
Paekchŏn	白川	996	3167	8477	4/9	3768	4709	44.44
Pongsan	鳳山	1564	6200	13,343		1040	12,303	7.79
Sohŭng	瑞興	1446	4337	8800		105	8695	1.19
Songhwa	松禾	685	1945	7088	1/4	1772	5316	25.00
Suan	遂安	1085	3786	6987		56	6931	0.80
Sinŭn	新恩	808	3189	9256		84	9172	0.91
Sinch'ŏn	信川	936	3081	12,002	1/3	4001	8001	33.33
Anak	安岳	991	3703	8839	1/4	2210	6629	25.00
Yonan	延安	1583	3718	9715	5/9	5397	4318	55.56
Ongchin	甕津	327	985	4016	1/5	803	3213	20.00
Ubong	牛峯	778	2180	6820		55	6765	0.81
Ŭnyul	殷栗	392	1143	3887	1/5	777	3110	20.00
Changyŏn	長淵	964	2104	16,668		904	15,764	5.42
Changyŏn	長連	330	874	2235	1/7	319	1916	14.29
Chaeyŏng	載寧	1293	3885	15,726	1/8	1966	13,760	12.50
T'osan	兎山	376	1186	2033		33	2000	1.62
Pyŏngsan	平山	2130	6323	20,727	1/10	2073	18,654	10.00
Pungch'ŏn	豊川	339	992	4711	1/9	523	4188	11.11
Haechu	海州	1926	6814	28,919	1/5	5784	23,135	20.00
Hwangchu	黃州	2034	5291	13,113		1100	12,013	8.39

(continued)

Table C.1 (continued)

Kangwŏn province		Households	Population	Arable land unit: Myŏck (結)	Ratio of wet field	Wetfield (Kyŏl)	Dryfield (Kyŏl)	The ratio of wet field (%)
Kangnŭng	江陵	1025	3513	5766	1/3	1922	3844	33.33
Yangyang	襄陽	857	1277	1833	2/5	733	1100	40.00
Chŏngsŏn	旌善	203	459	1005		1	1004	0.10
Pyŏngch'ang	平昌	233	501	1078		11	1067	1.02
wŏnchu	原州	1148	3233	7556	1/5	1511	6045	20.00
Yŏngwŏl	寧越	324	611	1463		8	1455	0.55
Hoengsŏng	橫城	313	595	2737	1/10	274	2463	10.00
Hongch'ŏn	洪川	420	1154	5579		148	5431	2.65
Hoeyang	淮陽	222	592	4586		7	4579	0.15
Kŭmsŏng	金城	340	759	3938		12	3926	0.30
Kŭmhwa	金化	181	517	3288		143	3145	4.35
Pyŏnggang	平康	163	212	3778		58	3720	1.54
Ichŏn	伊川	333	582	3310		8	3302	0.24
Samch'ŏk	三陟	581	2613	1998	1/8	250	1748	12.50
Pyŏnghae	平海	247	911	940	1/2	470	470	50.00
Ulchin	蔚珍	270	1483	1351	1/3	450	901	33.33
Chunch'ŏn	春川	1119	1950	5737	1/10	574	5163	10.00
Rangch'ŏn	狼川	264	750	1884		49	1835	2.60
Yanggu	楊口	297	641	1797		103	1694	5.73
Inche	麟蹄	125	207	1233		14	1219	1.14
Kansŏng	杆城	227	313	1302	1/2	651	651	50.00
Kosŏng	高城	375	871	1316		370	946	28.12
T'ongchŏn	通川	290	1363	1810	1/4	453	1358	25.00
Hŭpgok	歙谷	219	675	623	1/3	208	415	33.33

(continued)

Table C.1 (continued)

Pyŏngan province		Households	Population	Arable land unit: Myŏck (結)	Ratio of wet field	Wetfield (Kyŏl)	Dryfield (Kyŏl)	The ratio of wet field (%)
Pyŏngyang	平壤	1825	14,440	48,160	1/8	6020	42,140	12.50
Chunghwa	中和	1503	2710	13,895	1/8	1737	12,158	12.50
Sangwŏn	祥原	703	1899	6847		154	6693	2.25
Sangdŭng	三登	375	742	2527		8	2519	0.32
Kangdong	江東	894	1823	8031		145	7886	1.81
Sunan	順安	664	1751	5243	1/10	524	4719	10.00
Chŭngsan	甑山	301	835	2228	1/4	557	1671	25.00
Hamchong	咸從	807	1539	4359	1/4	1090	3269	25.00
Samhwa	三和	410	3105	4363	1/9	485	3878	11.11
Kangsŏ	江西	986	1699	4931	1/4	1233	3698	25.00
Yonggang	龍岡	1724	2643	8442	1/7	1206	7236	14.29
Anchu	安州	2690	8567	12,980	1/6	2163	10,817	16.67
Sŏngch'ŏn	成川	1068	2999	9714		57	9657	0.59
Sukch'ŏn	肅川	1318	1855	9208	1/3	3069	6139	33.33
Chansan	慈山	591	1181	6878		460	6418	6.69
Sunch'ŏn	順川	602	1741	8731		98	8633	1.12
Kaech'ŏn	价川	1200	5439	10,280		185	10,095	1.80
Tŏkch'ŏn	德川	881	3716	6039		–	6039	0.00
Yŏngyu	永柔	816	2171	7138	1/3	2379	4759	33.33
Maengsan	孟山	354	907	2862		–	2862	0.00
Ŭnsan	殷山	612	1200	6846		230	6616	3.36
Yangdŏk	陽德	325	952	4733		3	4730	0.06
Ŭichu	襄州	531	1498	7178		20	7158	0.28
Chŏngchu	定州	1033	5466	10,254	1/5	2051	8203	20.00
Insan	麟山	138	323	1444	1/10	144	1300	10.00

(continued)

Table C.1 (continued)

Pyŏngan province		Households	Population	Arable land unit: Myŏk (結)	Ratio of wet field	Wetfield (Kyŏl)	Dryfield (Kyŏl)	The ratio of wet field (%)
Yongch'ŏn	龍川	379	1132	8318	1/3	2773	5545	33.33
Ch'ŏlsan	鐵山	234	659	3702		455	3247	12.29
Kwaksan	郭山	302	2481	2654	1/5	531	2123	20.00
Such'ŏn	隨川	527	3108	3372	1/6	562	2810	16.67
Sŏnch'ŏn	宣川	528	4417	8146	1/8	1018	7128	12.50
Kasan	嘉山	473	1756	3371	1/3	1124	2247	33.33
Chŏngryŏng	定寧	297	839	2906		12	2894	0.41
Kanggye	江界	604	4248	11,309		7	11,302	0.06
Isan	理山	577	1686	6454		0	6454	0.01
Huich'ŏn	熙川	319	1060	5737		—	5737	0.00
Yŏyŏn	閭延	262	1573	785		1	784	0.13
Chasŏng	慈城	405	2576	1497		—	1497	0.00
Much'angŏ	茂昌	127	291	698		—	698	0.00
Uye	虞芮	77	331	518		—	518	0.00
Wiwŏn	渭源	217	1544	1650		1	1649	0.06
Sakchu	朔州	222	394	3583		—	3583	0.00
Yŏngbyŏn	寧邊	1121	2906	14,625		306	14,319	2.09
Ch'angsŏng	昌城	335	2200	2005		—	2005	0.00
Pŏkdong	碧潼	416	2726	2749		—	2749	0.00
Unsan	雲山	225	2763	4354		2	4352	0.05
Pakchŏn	博川	599	1035	3942	1/3	1314	2628	33.33
T'aechŏn	泰川	278	615	6084		120	5964	1.97

(continued)

Table C.1 (continued)

Hamgyŏng province		Households	Population	Arable land unit: Myŏck (結)	Ratio of wet field	Wetfield (Kyŏl)	Dryfield (Kyŏl)	The ratio of wet field (%)
Hamhŭng	咸興	3538	8913	27,774		850	26,924	3.06
Chŏngpyŏng	定平	811	3819	10,647	1/9	1183	9464	11.11
Pukchŏng	北靑	1539	4459	11,044		346	10,698	3.13
Yŏnghŭng	永興	2191	8524	10,529		570	9959	5.41
Kowŏn	高原	635	1178	5981		300	5681	5.02
Munchŏn	文川	450	953	3103	1/10	310	2793	10.00
Yewŏn	預原	494	2698	3682	1/7	526	3156	14.29
Anbyŏn	安邊	1030	3997	13,957	1/10	1396	12,561	10.00
Sŏnchŏn	端川	303	850	4446	1/8	556	3890	12.50
Yongchim	龍津	187	882	2067	1/10	207	1860	10.00
Kilchu	吉州	1673	14,819	12,833		335	12,498	2.61
Kyŏngwŏn	慶源	291	3233	2182		50	2132	2.29
Tanchŏn	宣川	832	2731	9277		334	8943	3.60
Kapsan	甲山	356	891	3940		—	3940	0.00
Kyŏngsŏng	鏡城	409	9031	8944		74	8870	0.83
Kyŏngwŏn	慶源	1162	5271	4096		10	4086	0.24
Hoeryŏng	會寧	624	2157	3853		12	3841	0.31
Chongsŏng	鍾城	900	21,815	4347		45	4302	1.04
Ŭnsŏng	穩城	800	3637	2970		9	2961	0.30
Kyŏnghŭng	慶興	402	5058	2283		1	2282	0.04
Puryŏng	富寧	262	2294	2913		—	2913	0.00
Samsu	三水	113	348	620		—	620	0.00

Appendix D: Glossary

Itu pronounce	Hangŭl	Itu Chinese	Meaning
baemi	배미	夜味	A strip of paddy field, a parcel of rice field
bb'ŏl	뻘	浌	Tideland
binu	비누	飛陋	Soap
bit	빛	色	Financial model color formatting
bok	복	洑	Dammed pool for irrigation
chang-i	쟁이	尺	Artisan
chil	질	作	Account personification
chilŭm	지름 기름	長音	Oil
chim	짐	卜	100 chim = 1 myŏck the land tax unit based on yield, original meaning is burden carrier
chŏkŭm	적음	題音	Writing
chum	줌	把	10 chum = 1 mukk the land tax unit based on yield, original meaning is handful
dulŭm	두름	冬音	A string (of fish)
hop	홉	合	A measure of capacity about 0.06 liter grain, 10 hop = 1 toe
chamkal	참갈	眞檪	A oak branches with leaves
k'i	키	箕	A tool used to separate grain from the chaff
kkŭlgae	끌개	曳介	Rake
koŭmp'a	곰방메	古音波	A mallet

APPENDIX D: GLOSSARY

Itu pronounce	Hangŭl	Itu Chinese	Meaning	
kŭlugali	그루갈이	根耕	Cultivating for root nodules of legume crops	
machiki	마지기	斗落	Sowing area for 6 liter seed	
mal	말	斗	A measure of capacity about 6 liter grain, 15 mal = 1 sŏm	
malguyu	말구유	馬槽	A trough	
malŭnsalmi	마른삶이	乾沙彌	Cultivating without water	
marŭm	마름	舍音	Supervisor of a tenant farm	
milgae	밀개	推介	A rake	
mukk	뭇	束	10 mukk = 1 chim the land tax unit based on yield, original meaning is to bind	
musalmi	무삶이	水沙彌	Cultivating with water	
myojong (苗種)	묘종	苗種	Seedling	
myŏk	역	結	The land tax unit based on yield, original meaning is bound collection of grain	
nalgae	날개	飛介	Straw mat	
nalgal-i	날가리	日耕	The size of field or paddy that takes a day's ox plowing	
Nat	낫	鎌	A sickle	
nŭtbyŏ	늦벼, 느린벼	晚稻	Late sowing rice	
olbyŏ, ilŭnbyŏ	올벼, 이른벼	早稻	Early sowing rice	
ondol	온돌	溫突	Provide the heating for a home and for cooking	
p'at	팥	小豆	Azuki (Red beans)	
p'at-binu	팥비누	小豆飛陋	Azuki (Red beans) soap	
pinsŏm	빈섬	空石	Straw basket	Store seed securely against moisture
pŏnchi	번지	翻地	A rake	
Sha	샤	夕	A measure of capacity about 0.006 liter grain, 10 sha = 1 hop	
soeshiryang	쇠스랑	手愁音	A pitchfork	
sŏm	섬	苫	Refers to a sŏm of rice for a straw bag	
sŏm	섬	石	A measure of capacity about 90 liter grain	
sŏmchiki	섬지기	石落	Sowing area about 90 liters seed	area for 90 liter seed
soshirang	소시랑	鐵齒擺	Pitchfork	
ssia	씨아	用良	Cotton gin	
ssŏhŭre	써레	所訖羅	A harrow	
tachim	다짐	侤	Bill	
tachim	다짐	侤音	Making a resolution	
tae	콩	太	Soybean	

APPENDIX D: GLOSSARY

Itu pronounce	Hangŭl	Itu Chinese	Meaning
toe	되	升	A measure of capacity about 0.6 liter grain, 10 toe = 1 mal
toechiki	되지기	升落	Sowing area for 0.6 liter seed
torikkae	도리깨	栲栳	A flail
ttabi	따비	地寶	A weeder plow
pŭnjong	번종	反種	A method is for wet fields which face a water shortage
halmikkot	할미꽃	白頭翁草	Korean pasque flower
mebyŏ	메벼	山稻	Mountainous rice
chokchong	족종	足種	Press the ground with the heel resting on a pit and the planting of seeds
chaenggi	쟁기	耒	Plough
pukchi	북지	北枝	Stirrups
chŏmmulgok	저물곡	占勿谷	A late-sowing quick-ripening variety of Proso/foxtail millet
saengdongchŏm	생동점	生動粘	A late-sowing quick-ripening variety of Proso/foxtail millet
tangsŏ	당서	唐黍	Sorghum
Kangjik]	강직	姜稷	A late-sowing quick-ripening variety of Barnyard Grass
Bomgali	봄갈이	春耕	The early-sowing variety of Soybeans, Red Beans, and Mung Beans
Kŭlugali	그루갈이	根耕	Refers to "the vernacular name for plowing with the roots still in the soil for root nodules of legume crops"
tongbae	동배동두	同輩	Saber bean
t'achack	타작	輾	Mill
chamk'ae	참깨	眞荏子	Sesamum
tŭlkkae	들깨	水荏子	Perilla
memil	메밀	木麥	Buckwheat

REFERENCES

Angus Maddison. *The World Economy: A Millennial Perspective*. Paris: Development Centre of the Organisation for Economic Co-operation and Development, 2007.

Bagrow Stockholm. The Maps from the Home Archives of the Descendants of a friend of Marco Polo. *Imago Mundi*, Vol. 5, pp. 3–13, 1948.

F. Dentener, et al. The Global Atmospheric Environment for the Next Generation. *Environmental Science and Technology*, Vol. 40, No. 11, pp. 3586–3594, 2006.

F. Niyi Akinnaso. The Consequences of Literacy in Pragmatic and Theoretical Perspectives. *Anthropology & Education Quarterly*, Vol. 12, No. 3, pp. 163–200, 1981.

F. H. King. *Farmers of Forty Centuries, or Permanent Agriculture in China, Korea and Japan*. Madison, 1911.

German Kim. Koryo Saram: Koreans in the Former. *USSR Korean and Korean American Studies Bulletin*, Vol. 12, Nos. 2/3, 2001.

German Kim. *Ethnic Enterpreneurship of Koreans in the USSR and Post Soviet and Central Asia* (No. 445). Institute of Developing Economies Japan External Trade Organization, 2009.

Ho-chol Lee. Agriculture as a Generator of Change in Late Choson Korea. *Nongop kyongje yongu*, Vol. 35, No. 1, pp. 173–197, 1994.

Ho-chul Lee. The Development of Agriculture and Society in Late Choson Dynasty, 1700–1870 (Kyongbuk taehakkyo nongop kwahak kisul yonguso). *Kyongbuk tae nonghakchi*, Vol. 13, pp. 1–7, 1995.

Ho-chul Lee. Agriculture as a Generator of Change in Late Choson Korea. In *The Last Stand of Asian Autonomies: Responses to Modernity in the Diverse States of Southeast Asia and Korea, 1750–1900*. Edited by Anthony Reid. New York: St. Martin's Press, 1997.

Ho-chul Lee. A Review of Korean Landownership System from the Choson Dynasty. *Nongop kyongje yongu*, Vol. 41, No. 4, pp. 77–107, 2000.

In-Taek Oh. The Method of Plowing and Seeding in the Cultivation Seen Through Nongso-chipyo (農書輯要) in the Early Chosŏn Dynasty. *Society and History*, Vol. 2, pp. 87–118, 1999.

In-Taek Oh. The Making of Dry Farming Area on Wet Field and the Characteristics of the Dry Farming System in the 18th and 19th Centuries. *Journal of Agricultural History*, Vol. 2, No. 2 (Korea Agricultural History Association), pp. 65–78, 2003.

J. Brewer and R. Porter, eds. *Consumption and the World of Goods*. London: Routledge, 1993.

Jan De Vries. The Industrial Revolution and the Industrious Revolution. *The Journal of Economic History*, Vol. 54, No. 2, pp. 249–270, June 1994.

Jan De Vries. *The Industrious Revolution: Consumer Behavior and the Household Economy, 1650 to the Present*. New York: Cambridge University Press, 2008.

Jane Kate Leonard. *Metals, Monies, and Markets in Early Modern Societies: East Asian and Global Perspectives*. Monies, Market, and Finance in China and East Asia, Vol 1. BUNKA - WENHUA. Tubinger Ostasiatische Forschungen. Tuebingen East Asian Studies (17), 2008.

Ja-Ock Guh and Yong In Kuk. Weeding Hypothesis on Direct Seeding Rice Field as Applied by the Old Firing and Water Dressing Method. *Korean Journal of Weed Science*, Vol. 31, No. 1, pp. 1–7, 2011.

Ja-Ock Guh, Eun-woong Lee, and Byong-Lyol Lee. Improvements of Rice Culture and Breeding Technology in Korea—Through the Recent 100 Years—The 8th International Conference of the East-Asian Agricultural History. Minami Kyushu University, Miyazaki, Japan, September 2008.

Jean de Vries. *The Industrious Revolution Consumer Behavior and the Household Economy, 1650 to the Present*. New York: Cambridge University Press, 2008.

Jing-shen Tao. *The Jurchen in Twelfth-Century China: A Study of Sinicization*. Seattle: University of Washington Press, 1976.

Jun Seong Ho. *A History of Rice Price in Late Chosŏn: 1725–1875*. Ph. D. Dissertation. Sung Kyun Kwan University (『조선후기 米價史 연구: 1725–1875』). 1998.

Jun Seong Ho. Monetary Authority Independence and Stability in Medieval Korea: The Koryŏ Monetary System Through Four Centuries of East Asian Transformations, 918–1392. *Financial History Review*, Vol. 21, No. 3, pp. 259–280, December 2014.

Jun Seong Ho and Evelyn Ruiz Gamarra. A Story of Globally Important Agricultural Wisdom in the 15th Century Chosŏn Korea. *Anthropology*, Vol. 6, No. 2, pp. 1–6, 2018.

Jun Seong Ho and James B. Lewis. Wages, Rents, and Interest Rates in Southern Korea, 1700 to 1900. In *Research in Economic History*. Edited by Alexander J. Field, Gregory Clark, and William Sundstrom, Vol. 24. Amsterdam: Elsevier, 2007.

Jun Seong Ho and James B. Lewis. Korean Expansion and Decline from the Seventeenth to the Nineteenth Century: A View Suggested by Adam Smith. *Journal of Economic History*, Vol. 68, No. 1, pp. 244–282, 2008.

Jun Seong Ho and James B. Lewis. Stability or Decline? Demand or Supply? *The Journal of Economic History*, Vol. 69, No. 4, pp. 1144–1151, 2009.

Jung Jin Shin. Special Section1: Genealogy of Humanities in East Asia; A Study on the Genealogy of "Grain Lexicon" Source Books and the Basic Analysis of Their Grain Lexicon List. *Journal of East Asian Cultures*, Vol. 54, pp. 67–95, 2013.

Kaoru Sugihara. The East Asian path of Economic Development: A Long-Term Perspective. In *The Resurgence of East Asia 500, 150 and 50 Year Perspectives*, Chapter 3, pp. 78–123. Edited by Giovanni Arrighi, Takeshi Hamashita, and Mark Selden. London: RoutledgeCurzon, 2003.

Karl A. Wittgogel. *History of Chinese Society Liao (907–1125)* American Philosophical Society, 1946.

Kenjiro Yoneda (米川賢次郎). Chi Min Yao Shu (A Guide to Agriculture and Animal Husbandry) and the System of Three Crops Per Two Years (齊民要術と二年三毛作) 東洋史研究, Vol. 17, No. 4, pp. 407–430, 1959.

Kenneth Pomeranz. *The Great Divergence China, Europe, and the Making of the Modern World Economy*. Princeton: Princeton University Press, 2000.

Kevin H. O'Rourke. *Power and Plenty Trade, War, and the World Economy in the Second Millennium*. Princeton and Oxford: Princeton University Press, 2007.

Kim Yong-sŏp. The First Discussion of Cotton Growing Method in the Later Editions of the Nongsa-Jiksol (農事直說) and Sashi-Ch'an'yo (四時纂要). *Tongbang Hakchi* (Journal of Korean Studies), Vol. 141, pp. 95–102, 1988.

Koohafkan and Altieri. *Globally Important Agricultural Heritage Systems: A Legacy for the Future*. Rome: Food and Agriculture Organization of the United Nations, 2011.

Kuiinuma Jirō (飯沼二郎). Introduction. In Takahashi, Noboru (高橋昇). *Chōsen hantō no nōhō to nōmin* (朝鮮半島の農法と農民). Edited by Kuiinuma Jirō (飯沼二郎), Takahashi Kōshirō (高橋甲四郎), and Miyajima Hiroshi (宮嶋博史). Tokyo: Miraisha (未來社), 1998 reprint of 1933–1937.

Lee Jung-chul. Petty Peasantry, and Transplanting of Joseon Dynasty in the Eighteen Century. *Hanguksahakbo*, Vol. 8, pp. 335–365, 2000.

M. Berg and K. Bruland, eds. *Technological Revolutions in Europe: Historical Perspectives.* Cheltenham, 1998.

M. Berg and H. Clifford, eds. *Consumers and Luxury: Consumer Culture in Europe, 1650–1850.* Manchester, 1999.

Mark Elvin. *Pattern of the Chinese Past: A Social and Economic Interpretation.* Stanford: Stanford University Press, 1973.

Maurice Courant. Introduction to the Bibliographie Coreenne. *Transactions of the Korea Branch of the Royal Asiatic Society,* Vol. 25, pp. 1–100, 1936.

Trollope Mark Napier. Book Production and Printing in Corea. *Transactions of the Korea Branch of the Royal Asiatic Society,* Vol. 25, pp. 101–107, 1936.

Maxine Berg. From Imitation to Invention: Creating Commodities in Eighteenth-Century Britain. *The Economic History Review,* New Series, Vol. 55, No. 1, pp. 1–30, 2002.

Min Seong-ki. A Study of the Ploughs of the Yi-Dynasty. *Yŏksahakbo,* Vol. 87, pp. 145–169, 1980.

Miyajima Hiroshi (宮嶋博史), 朝鮮農業史における15世紀朝鮮史叢, Vol. 3, pp. 3–83, June 1980.

Nagahara Keiji and Kozo Yamamura. Shaping the Process of Unification: Technological Progress in Sixteenth-and 17th-Century Japan. *Journal of Japanese Studies,* Vol. 14, No. 1, pp. 77–109, 1988.

Osamu Saito. Work Leisure and the Concept of Planning in the Japanese Past 1996. Labour-Intensive Industrialisation in Global History. Presented to the 13th International Economic History Congress, Buenos Aires 26th July 2002.

Peng Xinwei. *A Monetary History of China,* Vol. 2. Translated by Edward H. Kaplan. Western Washington University, 1994.

Peter Lee. *A History of Korean Literature.* Cambridge, UK: Cambridge University Press, 2003.

Ping-Ti Ho. Early-Ripening Rice in Chinese History. *The Economic History Review,* Vol. 9, No. 2, pp. 200–218, 1956.

R. Bean, B. W. Olesen, and K. W. Kim. History of Radiant Heating & Cooling Systems: Part 1. *ASHRAE Journal,* Vol. 14, pp. 40–47, 2010.

Randolph Barker. The Origin and Spread of Early-Sowing Champa Rice: It's Impact on Song Dynasty China. *Rice,* Vol. 4, No. 3, pp. 184–186, 2011.

Shiri Avnerya, Denise L. Mauzerallb, Junfeng Liuc, and Larry W. Horowitzc. Global Crop Yield Reductions Due to Surface Ozone Exposure: 2. Year 2030 Potential Crop Production Losses and Economic Damage Under Two Scenarios of O3 Pollution. *Atmospheric Environment,* Vol. 45, No. 13, pp. 2297–2309, 2011.

Sŏ Chŏngsang. Agricultural Technique of Nong-sa-jik-seol (農事直說) and the Identity of No-nong (老農). *Taedongkochŏnyŏngu* (泰東古典研究), Vol. 16, pp. 43–84, 1999.

Soh Soon-Yeol and Yu Chan-Ju. Formation of Farmer's Networking and Its Function for Regional Agricultural Development—A Case Study of the 'Rice Direct-Seeding Research Association'. *Journal of Regional Studies Chiyŏksahoiyŏngu*, Vol. 12, No. 1, pp. 91–111, 2004.

Sun Ah Lee and Soon Yeol Soh. The Publication Agricultural Books and Jeola Province Jeollado. *Nongŏpsayŏngu* (農業史研究), Vol. 5, No. 1, pp. 33–48, 2006.

Surendra K. Pradhan, Jarmo K. Holopainen, and Helvi Heinonen-Tanski. Stored Human Urine Supplemented with Wood Ash as Fertilizer in Tomato (*Solanum lycopersicum*) Cultivation and Its Impacts on Fruit Yield and Quality. *Journal of Agriculture Food Chemistry*, Vol. 57, No. 16, pp. 7612–7617, 2009.

T. Giovanni Arrighi, Takeshi Hamashita, and Mark Selden, eds. *The Resurgence of East Asia 500, 150 and 50 Year Perspectives*. London: RoutledgeCurzon, 2004.

Takahashi Noboru. *The Farmers and Farming Techniques of the Korean Peninsula* (Chosŏnbando ŭi nongbŏp kwa nongmin). Minsokwŏn, 1998.

Takahashi Noboru (高橋昇). *Chōsen hantō no nōhō to nōmin* (朝鮮半島の農法と農民). Edited by Kuiinuma Jirō (飯沼二郎), Takahashi Kōshirō (高橋甲四郎), and Miyajima Hiroshi (宮嶋博史). Tokyo: Miraisha (未來社), 1998 reprint of 1933–1937.

Takeda Shōchishiro. (武川統七郎) 實驗麥作新說 Tokyo (東京) Meibundo (明文堂), 1929.

The Travels of Marco Polo. The Complete Yule-Cordier Edition, Vols. 1 and 2. New York: Dover Publications, Inc., 1993.

Valeriy S. Khan. The Contributions of Koreans to the Socio-Economic Development and Culture of Central Asia, 3rd World Congress of Korean Studies, History Session 4, The Academy of Korean Studies Seoul, 2011.

Vijay Singh Meena, et al. *Potassium Solubilizing Microorganisms for Sustainable Agriculture*. Cham, Switzerland: Springer Nature, 2018.

William Wayne Farris. *Daily Life and Demographics in Ancient Japan*. Michigan Monograph Series in Japanese Studies (No. 63), 2009.

Wi Ŭnsuk. Koryo Period Farming Techniques and Productivity Research (Koryŏ sidae nongŏp kisul kwa saengsanyŏk yŏngu). *Kuksagwan Nonŏp*, Vol. 17, No. 1–26, 1990.

INDEX

A
Aged manure, 89, 94, 98, 101, 103, 107, 109
Agricultural revolution/Agriculture revolution, 5, 45
Alaska, 57
Aleutian Islands, 57
Ancient times, 79
Arable land, 25, 26, 31, 32, 42, 57, 69
Ash, 56, 57, 94, 98, 101, 103, 107, 109, 110
Attributability, 76
Autumn Equinox, 105, 109

B
Balhae, 104
Barley, 25, 34, 45, 48, 49, 56, 59–61, 68, 82, 98, 101–108
Barren, 83, 89, 94, 98, 101, 103–106, 109, 112
Biofertilizers, 55
Biological diversity, 3, 4, 16
Black Death, 6, 39
Bomgali, 103
Brim, 31, 82
Buddhist, 7, 15, 22
Bureau of Typecasting, 80

C
California School, 16
Chaff, 81, 90, 176, 184
Chamgal, 93
Chamkal, 91
Chim, 25
China, 4, 7, 14, 15, 18, 19, 22, 26, 27, 29, 33, 41, 42, 45, 46, 50, 55, 57, 58, 74, 76, 79, 80, 93, 108
Chosŏn dynasty, 15, 19–22, 42, 67, 68
Climatic change, 39, 43
Combination system, 34
Confucian/Confucianism, 4, 14–16, 18, 19, 22, 33, 41
Continuous system, 34
Copper coins, 22
Crops seed, 29
Cultural fusion, 5, 7, 29

D

Damp seeds, 81
Diminishing returns, 34
DMZ, 7
Drain, 88, 91–93
Drought, 21, 29, 40, 45, 48, 51, 52, 58, 60, 61, 87–91, 94
Drought-enduring, 55
Drought-resistant, 5, 52
Dry rice, 58–61, 178, 179

E

Early-ripening, 44, 49
Early-sowing, 34, 43–46, 48–50, 52, 58, 61, 62, 87–89, 91, 97, 103, 104
Earthenware jar, 29, 82
Embryo, 81
Envoys, 43

F

Farming tools, 46, 175
Fatal famines, 16
Feaces, 56
Fertilizer(s), 21, 60, 92, 94
Fiduciary power, 22
Fly droppings, 92
Food and Agriculture Organization (FAO), 3
Foreign affairs, 21
Foreign trade, 22
Furs, 7

G

Geographical Appendix of the Veritable Records of King Sejong (GAVK), 28, 42, 57, 69, 185
Global age, 15–17, 39
Global history, 4, 17
Globally Important Agricultural Heritage Systems (GIAHS), 67, 73
Gold, 7, 17, 21, 22
Grain in Ear, 89
Grains labeled, 51
Grain storage, 33–35
Great divergence, the, 4, 5
Greece, 7
Green peas, 34

H

Halmikkot, 93
Hamgyŏng Province, 29, 57
Hangŭl, 46, 49, 50, 61, 62, 74–76
Harvest, 26, 34, 40, 48, 49, 51, 52, 59, 87–89, 98, 99, 103–105, 107, 109, 112, 182
Hazelnuts, 111
Hemp, 25, 68, 81, 85, 86, 180
High-equilibrium trap, 46

I

Idu, 25, 75
Imitation-Innovation-Invention, 47, 48, 50, 74
Industrial revolution, 5, 47
Industrious revolution, 4, 45–48, 51
Infertile, 29, 56, 75, 89, 103
Infrastructure, 15, 33, 35
Intensive land use, 60
Intensive system, 34, 41
Intercropping, 18, 34, 60, 112
Irrigation, 33–35, 45, 63, 88

J

Japan, 4, 5, 14, 15, 18, 19, 29, 33, 39, 40, 49, 55, 56, 70
Japanese pirate, 18, 29
Jurchen/Jin, 5–7, 13, 14, 21, 26, 29

K
Kaesŏng, 7, 13–15
Kansho famine, 40
Khitan, 5, 7, 13, 14
Koguyŏ, 5, 25
Korea, 4–7, 14, 16–19, 21, 26–29, 32–34, 36, 40, 42, 45–51, 55, 56, 60–62, 68–70, 73, 75, 76, 89, 91
Koreana Tripitaka, 14
Koryo Saram, 3, 4
Kŭlugali, 59, 103, 104
Kuril, 7

L
Late-ripening, 44
Legume, 34, 45, 56, 59, 60
Leguminous plants, 55
Liao, 5, 7, 13, 14
Lowland, 4–6, 42

M
Majigi, 91
Malthusian trap, 4, 5
Malthusian virtue, 39
Malŭnsalmi, 58
Marco Polo, 7, 13, 15
Marŭnsami, 87
Mathusian virtue, 41
Medical Prescriptions, 20
Medieval, 13, 17, 18
Memil, 109
Microorganisms, 55
Milan, 15
Millet, 25, 34, 49, 60, 68, 97–99, 101, 104, 106
Ming, 5, 16, 18, 21, 22, 33, 43, 44
Miscellanies on Kŭmyang District (MKD), 16, 49, 50, 52, 70, 74, 75, 77
Mixed cropping, 18, 34

Moisture, 43, 81
Mongol, 14, 21, 22
Mongol Empire, 45
Mono-cultivation, 56
Morning, 16, 49
Mountainous rice, 93
Mukŭm, 25
Mung beans, 68, 83, 104, 106
Muromachi Era, 39
Musalmi, 58, 87
Myŏck, 25
Myojong, 58, 87

N
Nalgae, 31, 82, 177
Naples, 15
Natural calamities, 6
Natural nutrient, 55
New alphabet, 62
Night soil, 89, 91
Nitrogen, 56, 59, 91
Non-attributability, 76
Nongsa chiksŏl, 19, 59, 175
Non-permanence, 76
Northeast Asia, 5, 25
Nutrients, 52, 91

O
Offerings, 79
Ondol, 57
Oral culture, 75, 76
Ox, 19–21, 83, 95, 98, 99, 104, 112
Ozone, 73, 74

P
Paddies, 45, 57, 58, 60, 88, 178, 179
Paper money, 21, 22
Pastoral life, 5, 31
Permanence, 76
Persia, 7

Phosphorus, 91
Pirates, 16, 17, 29
Ploughing, 55
Plowed oxen, 18
Poetry, 80
Population growth, 5, 26, 27, 33, 35, 46
Portugal, 17
Potassium, 91
Productivity, 4, 5, 22, 33, 34, 36, 51, 56, 74
Property rights, 33–35
Pukchi, 95
Pŭnjong, 92

Q
Qing, 5, 6, 58

R
Rainfall, 5, 26, 34, 63, 92
Real Value of Land (RVL), 36
Ridges, 94, 97–99, 101, 102, 108, 111, 112
Roots, 55, 59, 91–93, 98, 99, 103–105, 107, 182
Rotation system, 34
Rotting, 92
Russia, 7

S
Sacks, 81, 82
Seasoned farmers, 16, 32, 41, 42, 46, 56, 80, 91, 93, 103, 118
Sedentary life, 5, 13
Seedlings, 34, 58, 87, 88, 90–93, 98
Sejong sillok chiriji, 69
Semiagricultural society, 32
Silkworm(s), 31, 89
Silver, 7, 21, 22

Sinitic civilization, 29
Sino-centric bias, 5, 6
Smithian virtue, 42
Snow, 29, 31, 32, 82
Soil acidity, 91
Soil nitrogen, 55, 103
Song, 5, 7, 13–15, 31, 45
Sorghum, 68, 97, 99
Sovereignty, 15, 22
Spain, 17
Sprouts, 82, 88, 94, 182
Stalin, 3
Standard of living, the, 4, 35
State monopoly, 22
Steppes, 3, 6
Storage pit, 82
Submerge, 81
Suitability, 82
Summer beans, 34
Syria, 7

T
Tamping, 86
Tang, 5, 108
Tartar, 7
Thaw, 83, 85, 87, 88
Timing, 44, 51, 79, 109
Toilets, 56
Transplanting, 68, 87, 90, 92, 93, 108
Transport, 34, 35
Trickle down theory, 76
Ttabi, 94

U
Ŭiju, 44
Unalaska, 57
Upland, 5, 6, 13, 25, 26, 29, 42, 56, 57, 68, 87, 118
Urban economies, 4
Urbanism, 15

Urine, 56, 82, 90, 92–94, 110, 112
Urine and ash fertilizer, 56, 89, 90, 111

V
Venice, 15
Veterinary book, 20

W
Winnowing, 81
Winter wheat, 34

Wooden tub, 29, 82
Written culture, 76

Y
Yuan, 5, 13

Z
Zeng He, 17
Zŭm, 25

Printed in the United States
By Bookmasters